FIRST EDITION

Published by Vantage Press, Inc.
516 West 34th Street, New York, New York 10001

Manufactured in the United States of America
ISBN: 0-533-12711- 4

Library of Congress Catalog Card No.: 98-90131

0 9 8 7 6 5 4 3 2 1

Contents

Preface

The Bible contains many types of writing. The Old Testament contains history, hymns, and drama. The Gospels are considered by many to be history. Some of Paul's writings are theological discourses. The Revelation stands by itself as a writing. It is an apocalypse. During the latter part of the Old Testament and first two centuries of the Christian era, there were many writings of this kind. They had a prophetic purpose. The Revelation belongs to this type of writing. The Revelation may be as a book considered a symbolic book to be deciphered. Authorship of these types of books were often ascribed to a person who lived many years before the writer.

Through the centuries, the Revelation was considered to have been written by John the disciple. The King James translation title of this book is "The Revelation of St. John the Divine." The majority of New Testament scholars today do not consider John as the writer. Some ascribed the writer to John the elder. Many in the early church did not rank this book on the authoritative plane of the Gospels. The Peshitta, fifth century Syriac version did not contain the Revelation. It may be said that in the West, the apostle's authorship was accepted by Justin Martyr (A.D. 150), Irenaeus (A.D. 180), and Tertullian in Africa (A.D. 200). The East never fully accepted this view. Usually they said that John wrote it, but not the disciple.

While the Revelation has been dated between 60 and 125, the majority accept the dates between 69 and 96. Although some scholars have dated the book during the reign of Nero

(54–68), it is more likely that it was written during the period of Domitian (81–96). Domitian required Caesar worship but excluded the Jews. Bishop Polycarp lived during the first half of the second century. His church in Smyrna did not exist after Paul's time. The church of Laodicea, described in Revelation 3:17, was completely described in A.D. 61.

It is interesting to observe that the Revelation has been the sole basis for the creation of church groups during the twentieth century while at the same time, some clergy in major denominations simply avoided its use. A wider perspective of this book may be gained by reading a few books of this type written during this period. Read Daniel 38 and 39, Zechariah 9–14, Isaiah 24–27: and outside the Old Testament, the Book of Enoch, the Fourth Book of Ezra, the Ascension of Isaiah, the Apocalypse of Zephaniah, and parts of the Sibylline Oracles. The historian Eusebius (A.D. 325) regarded the book as either "spurius" or "recognize." However, Athanasius of Alexandria in A.D. 367, and the later church fathers of the West regarded the book after the fourth century. The following diagrams, charts, and notes will help the interpretation of this book of Christian faith.

Dr. W. L. Ludlow's Outline of the Revelation

I. The title of the Revelation (1:1–3)
II. Salutation to the seven churches (1:4–6)
III. Prologue: Two voices (herald the Lord God) (1:7–8)
IV. <u>ACT I:</u> THE CHURCH ON EARTH (1:9–3:22)

A. Setting: The seven golden lampstands (1:9–20)
B. The letters to the seven churches (chapters 2 & 3)

VI. <u>ACT III:</u> THE CHURCH IN TRIBULATION (8:2–11:18)

A. Setting: The altars, prayers of the saints (8:2–6)
B. The sounding of the seven trumpets (8:7–11:18)

Scene 1: Hail and fire fall (8:7)
Scene 2: A mountain cast into the sea (8:8–9)
Scene 3: A star falls on rivers and springs (8:10–11)
Scene 4: Heavenly bodies darkened (8:12); and eagle announces three woes (8:13)
Scene 5: (Woe 1): Pit of the abyss; locusts (9:1–12)
Scene 6: (Woe 2): Four angels released (9:13–15); two hundred million horsemen (9:16–21); angel with the little book (10); times of the Gentiles, two prophets, the evil city (11:1–14)
Scene 7: (Woe 3): Worship in heaven (11:15–18)

VII. <u>ACT IV:</u> THE SALVATION OF THE CHURCH (11:19–15:4)

A. Setting: The ark of the covenant (11:19)
B. The showing of the seven pageants (12:1–15:4)

Scene 1: The woman and the dragon (12)
Scene 2: The beast arising from the sea (13:1–10)
Scene 3: The beast arising from the land (13:11–18)
Scene 4: The Lamb with the 144,000 martyrs (14:1–5)

Scene 2: The beast at war with the woman (17:6–18)
Scene 3: The final cosmic oratorio (18:1–19:10)
Scene 4: The Word of God on the white horse (19:11–16)
Scene 5: The angel standing in the sun (19:17–18)
Scene 6: The Battle of Armageddon (19:19–21)
Scene 7: Satan cast into the abyss (20:1–3)

X. ACT VII: THE CHURCH IN THE MILLENNIUM (20:4–2215)

A. Setting: The church enthroned with Christ. (20:4–Satan's limited authority and defeat. (20:7–10)
B. The fulfilling of God's sevenfold plan (20:11–22:5)

Scene 1: The old heaven and old earth. (20:11)
Scene 2: The Last Judgment. (20:12–15)
Scene 3: The new heaven and the new earth. (21:1)
Scene 4: The new Jerusalem. (21:2–8)
Scene 5: Measuring the city. (21:9–21)
Scene 6: The city's illumination. (21:22–27)
Scene 7: The city's source of light. (22:1–5)

XI. EPILOGUE: IMPRIMATURS OF THE BOOK (22:6–20)
XII. CLOSING BENEDICTION (22:21)

DIAGRAM OF REVELATION
For Those Explaining the Millennium Rule

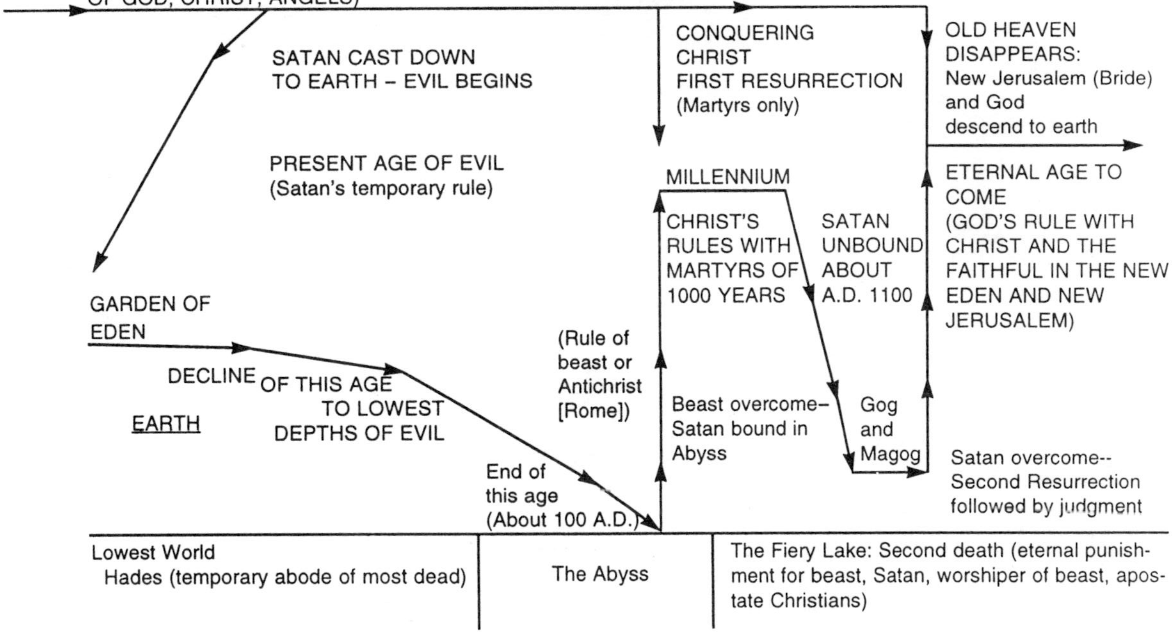

1

Christophany in the Revelation

The Revelation has six symphonic themes. These themes are of faith, hope and victory. No other thoughts are found in this book. These six symphonic themes are given in symbols. The text assigned for tonight contains one theme: JUDGMENT AND RENEWAL WITHIN THE HOUSE OF GOD ARE NEVER AN ISOLATED EXPERIENCE. IT IS THE WORLD THAT GOD IS SEEKING TO REDEEM. This theme comes to a climax in Part 2:4–11:15–19.

Two symphonic themes are found in Part 2, Chapters 4–11, 19. The Coming Kingdom of God is one Christophany. It has come in part; it is here in part but it is also coming in its fullest dimension. The other Christophany is the message of judgment.

Part three of Revelation consists of three Christophanies, Revelation 12–22. These three Christophanies are Rev. 12–14, "God's Purpose in Travail," Rev. 15–19:4, "The Song of Salvation;" and Rev. 19:5-22, 21, "The Great Hallelujah."

Each movement begins with a Christophany and moves through seven events. These events are seven in number and are described in units: 1) seven seals; 2) seven trumpets; 3) seven bowls; 4) seven blessings; 5) seven symbols of evil; 6) seven pictures of the Church.

It should be said that these units do not necessarily determine the basic pattern of the book, but they are blended into his overall design. He groups, for effect, those elements which belong to the same unit of seven, as in the case of the seals, trumpets, and bowls; whereas in the case of the seven benedictions or the seven symbols of evil or of the Church, John distributes them throughout the book, producing thereby the effect of repetition, or symmetry.

Throughout the Revelation there moves two designs, or strands. There is the realm of history, and then there is the realm of liturgy. The basic unit of time in this book is the week, and here John uses it as his key to unfold history. The week begins with Sunday, Rev. 1:10, "I was in the Spirit on the Lord's Day." This was the day on which Creation was begun. On this day light was created. The first vision of each of the six movements in the book of Revelation is set out as a Christophany. Christ is the light of the world. Now the visions on Creation Sunday are these: 1) Christ amidst the lamps, 2) The Lamb amidst the throne, 3) The Lord's people in supplication, 4) The dragon against the child, 5) The song of Moses and of the Lamb, 6) The Bridegroom of the Church.

All these visions are radiant with light. The <u>first</u> is illuminated by the seven-branch lamp of the temple, the <u>second</u> is set amidst the glory of the throne in heaven, the <u>third</u> is seen in the glow of the charcoal on the altar, the <u>fourth</u> is joined to the vision of the woman in light, the <u>fifth</u> is heard across the fire of the crystal sea, the <u>sixth</u> is bright with the beauty of the bride as she receives her Bridegroom.

Following each Christophany are visions which set forward the story of man's life as it is lived amidst the temptations of the world; the lure of earth to compromise one's faith, the call of God to repentance and to surrender. The events which these visions portray happen from Monday to Thursday. There is a fourfold symbolism used to tell their story.

The visions on Creation Sunday tell of events in heaven. The visions on the weekdays tell of events on earth. Four is the numeral symbol of earth. Visions on the four weekdays are these: 1) The four churches tempted to compromise (Ephesus, Smyrna, Pergamum, Thyatira); 2) The four horsemen revealing sin's nature; 3) The four trumpets calling to repentance; 4) The four monsters rebelling against God; 5) The four plagues executing judgment; 6) The four powers finally destroyed.

The primary units of the material John uses are in groups of seven, but these groups of seven are divided into 4 and 3—the four being taken together as given in above items, and the three being woven into the general movement separately.

Following the weekday visions come the visions on Friday. These have the cross as their motif. The events they picture take place on Calvary. They are events concerning the current temporary success of sin, the choice between life and death, the encounter between God and evil. Here are the Friday visions: 1) Sardis: Dying but called to life; 2) Martyrs: Their cry and its responses; 3) Eagle: The vulture to the corpse; 4) Branded: The mark of the beast and of the Lamb; 5) Armageddon: The last issue; 6) Gog and Magog: The final encounter.

The Friday visions contain the heart of John's message to the churches. In visions we are brought to the foot of the cross, there to see the meaning of their predicament and there to find encouragement for their faithfulness.

The Saturday visions are Sabbath visions. The Sabbath is, for a Christian, a day of promise. The Sabbath visions are visions of events that are pointed to the future. They are concerned with the proclaiming of redemption and the calling of the redeemed. They are concerned with the declaration of judgment and its execution. Saturday visions: 1) Philadelphia—summoned to its apostleship; 2) The host of the redeemed; 3) The gospel of redemption; 4) The nature of judgment; 5) The judgment of Rome; 6) The last judgment.

The Sabbath is the controlling by John's teaching. The

Sabbath points to work which now is unfulfilled, as well as what is to be done. However, the guarantee of this "rest" is the victory of Easter Day. John here begins with each movement as a Christophany on Creation Sunday and ends with a vision of "consummation" on Easter Sunday. Here are the visions on Easter Sunday: 1) Laodicea: The Lord knocks at the door; 2) The unsealed roll: The sons of God are revealed; 3) The last trumpet: The Kingdom comes; 4) The harvest reaped: The close of the age; 5) Lamentation: The great city is destroyed; 6) The eternal city.

The Jewish festival year represented a continuous movement of the history of Israel from the celebration of its deliverance from Egypt up to the fulfillment of its destiny according to God's promises to Abraham. John, here in <u>Revelation</u>, fulfills his design to set his visions within the perspective of history with symbols of development. They would be as follows:

1. <u>Passover:</u> The letters of John to the seven churches are concerned with the period of preparation. The churches must get ready for the feast. The Lord is now searching out with lamps the leaven in their midst. He will come and knock at the door. This search was made with lit candles. Then, on the day of Passover itself, was held the Passover meal.
2. <u>Pentecost:</u> The period from the Passover to Pentecost, seven weeks afterward, was one season. The chief events of the season were related to the birth of spring and gathering of the first fruits from the fields. The spring of Israel began with their deliverance from Egypt, which was an act of God Israel celebrated by the sacrifice of the Paschal lamb. Then came Pentecost, which was a thanksgiving festival for the harvest of fruits. On this day was

also celebrated the giving of the Law on Mount Sinai.

The second section of Revelation (with the visions of seals) we see the vision of the Paschal lamb, but it is not the lamb slain but the lamb is slain by His followers. It is their blood which, as in the Passover rite, is poured at the base of the altar. But Passover ends with Pentecost. Moses brought the tablets of the Law, Jesus breaks the seals of the scroll of Life. When the seals are broken, the sons of God are revealed. They are the first fruits of the new age.

3. New Year: The people of Israel had their stormy history. Under Ezra and Nehemiah a new day began. The festival of New Year celebrated this new day on the new-moon day of the seventh month. So the message of Revelation moves from Pentecost to New Year. Here the trumpets are sounding (Rev. 6:1–8:6). The open scroll is read. Prophecy bears witness, and the Kingdom comes.
4. Day of Atonement: The New Year began a period of fasting, on the tenth day of which came the Day of Atonement. Israel never forgot that in spite of the Law, they had broken it again and again. So, the final section of John's visions open with the vision of Him who came to atone. The dragon is out to destroy Him. But though the period when the wheat and tares grow together seems long, and those who bear the mark of the beast seem to rejoice over the sorrows of those who bear the mark of the Lamb the harvest for certain is coming (Rev. 8:7–11:19).
5. Tabernacles: This feast was the feast of the end of the harvest. It announced the great certainty of the

future; when Israel shall have completed its journey through the wilderness, and the nations of the world would be its fruit unto the Lord. Here in Revelation we see the visions of the bowls of God's wrath. The last sacrifice is the burning of evil.

6. Dedication: So the pilgrimage comes to an end. When Judae Maccabeus rededicated the altar after setting the people free, and then restored the worship of the Lord in the temple, it did seem that the new day had once again dawned. Israel celebrated this day as the Feast of Lights. So John closes his book with a benediction.

The great hallelujah is heard as the nations join together in Zion. The final battle is fought, and victory easily won. The last judgment is over, and the eternal city is founded. The Jewish festival year running from Passover to Dedication is fulfilled in the Christian story. At the Dedication, the old temple was restored. For worship at Christmas, the new temple was set in the midst of men. God had become flesh. The chief rite in the celebration of the Dedication festival was the lighting of the seven-fold lamp; the opening vision of John's message is the Christ as He stands in the midst of His Church. The feast of Dedication closed the Jewish festal year; Christmas begins the festal year for the Christian Church.

2

The Drama of the Book of Revelation

<u>Introduction:</u>

(a) John's title for His book (1:1–3)

(b) The Letter Form of This Apocalypse (1:4–6 and 22:21)

<u>The Drama of the Book of Revelation:</u>

Prologue (1:7–8)

<u>Act I</u>

"Vision of the Church on Earth" "The Son of Man in Its Midst" (1:9–3:22)

(The Letters to the Seven Churches)

<u>Act II</u>

"Vision of God in Heaven—God's Purpose in History" (4:1–9:1) (The Opening of the Seven Seals)

<u>Act III</u>

"Vision of the Seven Angels of the Presence—The Church in Tribulation" (8:2–11:18) (The Sounding of the Seven Trumpets)

<u>Act IV</u>

"Vision of the Church Triumphant—the Drama of Salvation" (11:19, 14:20 and 15:2–4) (The Showing of the Seven Pageants)

<u>Act V</u>

"Vision of the Seven Angels of God's Wrath—The World in Agony" (15:1–16, 21) (The Pouring Out of the Seven Bowls)

Act VI

"Vision of Babylon's Overthrow—The Drama of Judgement" (17:1–20:3 and 7–10) (The Unfolding of the Seven Plagues)

Act VII

"Vision of the Church in the Millennium—Consummation of God's Purpose" (20:4–6 and 20:11 to 22:5)

Epilogue: (22:6–20)

3

The Structure of The Revelation

The construction of The Revelation is unique. Here is one scheme, among many, which can show its very artistic arrangement. It is here a scheme of seven sevens is revealed in the Revelation.

Seven Series of Seven

The First Septet

After a preliminary section to the whole apocalypse (1:12–8) and an introduction to the first septet (1:9–20), there are seven prophecies to the seven churches:

1. Ephesus (2:1–7)
2. Smyra (2:8–11)
3. Pergamum (2:12–17)
4. Thyatira (2:18–19)
5. Sardis (3:1–6)
6. Philadelphia (3:7–13)
7. Laodicea (3:14–22)

The Second Septet

After chapters 4–5, which are introductory to the second septet, come the seven seals:

1. The white horse (6:1–2)
2. The red horse (6:3–4)
3. The black horse (6:5–6)
4. The yellowish-green horse (6:7–8)
5. The soul under the altar (6:9–11)
6. The earthquake (6:12–17)
7. Seems to comprise all of the third septet

The Third Septet

After a preparatory vision (8:1–6), the seven trumpets are sounded:

1. The earth is set on fire (8:7)
2. The sea is turned to blood (8:8–9)
3. The rivers and springs become bitter (8:10–11)
4. The heavenly bodies are dimmed (8:12–13)
5. The locusts (9:1–2)
6. The horsemen (9:13–11:14)
7. The seventh trumpet, seeming to comprise all of the fourth septet

The Fourth Septet

After an introductory section (11:6–19), seven signs appear:

1. The woman with child (12:1–2)
2. The dragon (12:3–6)
3. The beast rising out of the sea (13:1–10)

4. The beast rising out of the earth (13:11–18)
5. The Lamb and the virgins (14:1–5)
6. The seven angels, counting one like a son of man (14:6–20)
7. The seventh sign, seeming to comprise all of the fifth septet

The Fifth Septet

After an introductory section in 15:1–16:3), seven bowls of wrath are poured out:

1. On the earth (16:2)
2. On the sea (16:3)
3. On the waters (16:4–7)
4. On the sun (16:8–9)
5. On the throne of the beast (16:10–11)
6. On the Euphrates (16:12–16)
7. The seventh bowl, seeming to comprise all of the sixth septet

The Sixth Septet

After an introductory section (16:17–21) there are seven stages in the fall of Babylon:

1. The description of Babylon (17:1–6)
2. The explanation of Babylon (17:7–18)
3. The fall of Babylon (18:1–8)
4. The mourning of Babylon (18:9–20)
5. The final ruin of Babylon (18:21–24)
6. The song of praise at her fall (19:1–5)
7. The seventh stage, seeming to comprise all the seventh septet

The Seventh Septet

After an introductory section (19:6–10), there occur the following scenes:

1. Rider on the white horse (19:11–15)
2. Supper of God (19:17–18)
3. Capture of the two beasts (19:19–21)
4. Angel of the abyss (20:1–3)
5. First resurrection (20:4–10)
6. Judgment Scene (20:11–15)
7. The New Jerusalem (21:1–22:5)

Revelation 22:6–21 is a recapitulation and finale, but does not contain Christian additions and doublets.

The above was adapted by Dr. Ludlow from R. J. Loener Zop, The Apocalypse of St. John, translated by H. J. Carpenter (London: Sheed & Ward, 1947).

4

The Seven Beatitudes of Revelation

1. The seven beatitudes in the Book of Revelation are:

[I] Blessed is he who reads aloud the words of the prophecy, and blessed are those who hear, and who keep what is written therein; for the time is near. (Revelation 1:3)
[II] Blessed are the dead who die in the Lord henceforth. Blessed indeed, says the spirit, that they may rest from their labors, for their deeds follow them. (Revelation 14:13)
[III] Blessed is he who is awake, keeping his garments that he may not go naked and be seen exposed. (Revelation 16:15)
[IV] Blessed are those who are invited to the marriage supper of the Lamb. (Revelation 19:9)
[V] Blessed and holy is he who shares in the first resurrection. Over such the second death has no power, but they shall be priests of God and of Christ, and they shall reign with him a thousand years. (Revelation 20:6)
[VI] Blessed is he who keeps the words of the prophecy of this book. (Revelation 22:7)
[VII] Blessed are those who wash their robes, that they may have the right to the tree of life and that they may enter the city by the gates. (Revelation 22:14)

2. Dr. J. Merle Rife, former professor of the classics at Muskingum College, has observed that the Book of Revelation is like the Eastern Orthodox Church. It is Byzantine. First among its many characteristics is the feature of the Byzantine

liturgies. There chants and weird Byzantine psaltery. The orthodox churches are full of color and ornaments, and we find in the Apocalypse brass, white wool, fire, gold, stars, rainbows, black, red, white, and pale green horses, precious stones such as jasper, sapphires, chalcedony, emerald, sardonyx, sardius, beryl, topaz and other stones; transparent gold and a final burst of glory in which it is declared that the holy city, the New Jerusalem, has no need of the sun or moon to light it, for the Lord God and the Lamb are its light. The bright vestments of orthodox clergy are more than matched by the woman whom the seer sees dressed in the sun. Like orthodox rituals, Revelation is full of dramatic action. In the liturgy, as in the flow of drama in Revelation, there are processions, the little and great entrances, much moving about of the clergy and acolytes, members of the congregation are in motion kissing icons, lighting candles, making the sign of the cross, while little children often run about in the back of the church. So is the action in Revelation: Horses and riders go out to war, angels are seen flying, a great dragon pursues a woman and she is given the wings of an eagle and flies away into the desert, seven bowls of wrath are poured out on the earth, beasts come up out of the earth and out of the sea, armies of good and evil are arrayed for the greatest of all world wars, there are earthquakes, the sun and moon are convulsed, the sky is rolled up like a scroll, and after all these mighty upheavals the holy city, even the New Jerusalem, comes down out of heaven like a bride adorned for her husband. The Revelation is a masterpiece of impressionistic art, something to be felt rather than to be talked about.

3. Beatitude No. 1: Five things may be said about this beatitude: 1) Revelation begins with God. God is the fountain of all truth. Every truth which individuals have comes from two sources: (a) discovery of the human mind; (b) gift of God. 2) God gives this revelation to Jesus Christ. 3) Jesus sent the truth

through John. 4) God must find those individuals into whose minds He can entrust His truth. 5) Content and message of the book of Revelation is to happen quickly. A summary title for beatitude number one is: "The Blessed of reading, hearing and obeying the Word of God."

4. Beatitude No. 2: The sounding of the seven trumpet woes (Rev. 8:7–11:19) is intended to bring all the people to repentance. Before this, however, is the silence and thunder of prayer (Rev. 8:1–5). The message is that "God can always hear the whispered prayer of the humblest of His praying and trusting people." God can use nature to send His messages. Three thoughts emerge out of the chapters from which this beatitude comes: 1) Whatever God has ordained for a person, that must be accepted. 2) Anyone who takes the sword will perish by it, for love cannot be defended by violence. 3) Weapons which Christians must use are endurance and faith. A summary title for beatitude number 2 is: "Blessedness in heaven of Christ's friends on earth."

5. Beatitude No. 3: Between this beatitude and number 2 is the 15th chapter and part of the 16th which picture seven angels, with seven plagues, who sing martyr songs and are given seven bowls filled with the wrath of God. This represents God's wrath against all sin. John may have had Leviticus 26:2 in mind when he wrote this. At Armageddon (or Hermagedon as Moffatt and a few others would have it), the forces of God will meet with the forces of Satan with the result that God will win. A title summary of this beatitude is: "The blessedness of the watchful pilgrim."

6. Beatitude No. 4: Who are the "invited" to the marriage supper of the Lamb? Obviously they are the faithful who refused to worship "Babylon-Rome." The harlot in chapters 17

and 18 is Rome. The beast are the institutions in Rome contributing to evil. Verses 6–8 of chapter 18 Barclay titled "The Doom of Pride." It contains two basic thoughts for Christian living: 1) What a person sows, that also will be reaped. 2) All pride and arrogance some day meets with the experience of being humiliated. "Pride goes before a fall." What is the title summary for this beatitude? It is this: "The blessedness of the invited guests of God."

7. Beatitude No. 5: The seven visions of John, which begin with Revelation 19:11, contain the final picture which might be titled: "The End of Satan's Evil Age and the Beginning of God's Righteous Age." The six sets of visions which preceded this last set contain a simple message in each of them. Here is a summary: 1) God has a purpose in history; His plans are supreme and sure (Rev. 6:1–8:6). 2) The Church of Jesus Christ will always be tested with evil. (Rev. 8:7–11, 19) 3) Paul's words in 2 Corinthians 4:17–18 are the explanation: "For this slight momentary affliction is preparing us an eternal weight of glory beyond all comparison, because we look not to the things that are seen but to the things that are unseen; for the things that are seen are transient, but the things that are unseen are eternal." 4) Again, Paul's words in Colossians 1:16–17 may be used, "For in him all things were created . . . all things were created through Him and for Him . . . and in Him all things hold together." 5) Punishment of God and redemption belong together, for they are the results of the same love. 6) The history of human civilization must be studied in the shadow of Babel. "Come let us build ourselves a city, and a tower with its top in the heavens . . . " (Genesis 11:4). Verse 6 in chapter 20 describes the privileges of the witnesses of Christ. They are three: 1) Death has no power over them. 2) These witnesses are priests of God (the Latin word, pontifex, priest, means bridge builder). 3) These witnesses are to live with

Christ. What, then, can we give as a summary title to beatitude number 5? It is this: "The gift of life everlasting, the gift of access to God, the privileges of bringing others to Jesus Christ, the gift of royalty,—these are the gifts which Jesus Christ gives to His own."

8. Beatitude No. 6: This beatitude reminds us of the words of the Prophet Isaiah: "Behold, I create new heavens and a new earth; and the former shall not be remembered, nor come into mind." (Isaiah 65:17) The Book of Enoch, which was read widely in the early church, has this passage: "I will transform the heaven and make it an eternal blessing and light; and I will transform the earth and make it a blessing." (Enoch 45:4) In his synagogue, the form of prayer every Jew still prays is this: "And to Jerusalem thy city return with compassion, and dwell therein as thou has promised; and rebuild her speedily; and the throne of David speedily establish there. Blessed art thou, O Lord, the builder of Jerusalem. " The New Jerusalem is then related to the new man. This sixth beatitude is a promise. There are three results which come from the observing of the commands of this Book of Revelation: (1) There is the river of the water of life. (Psalms 46:4, "The river whose streams make glad the city of our God.") (2) There is the tree of life. There is a Jewish legend which states this: "In any age to come God will create trees which will produce fruit in any month; and the man who eats from them will be healed." (3) The perfect city has not darkness, for the Presence and the light of God is there. Two comments should be given about the size of the city: 1) First, the size is given as 1,500 miles on each side with a wall 266 feet high. A city this size would stretch from London to New York City. What is symbolized here is that the New Jerusalem will be large enough for all the children of God. The precious stones described in Revelation 21:18–21 are interesting. It may be noted that eight of them are

the same as the stones on the breast-plate of the High Priest (Exodus 28:17). Furthermore, these stones are beyond price in value. Finally, the relationship between these stones and the signs of the Zodiac is interesting. In the east there was the idea of the city of the gods in the skies. There the gods dwelt. The sun and the moon and the stars were their lights. The Milky Way was their great street of the gods. There were twelve gates through which the stars went in and out upon their business. Now connected with the city of gods there are, of course, the signs of the Zodiac: the signs of the parts of the heaven through which the sun passes. The curious thing is that the signs of the zodiac have as their corresponding symbolic precious stones exactly these twelve stones. The table is as follows:

THE RAM—the amethyst
THE BULL—the jacinth
THE TWINS—the chrysopraso
THE CRAB—the topaz
THE LION—the beryl
THE VIRGIN—the chrysolite
THE BALANCE—the carnelian
THE SCORPION—the sardonyx
THE ARCHER—the emerald
THE GOAT—the chalcedony
THE WATER-CARRIER—the sapphire
THE FISHES—the jasper

There is a possibility that John was thinking of the city of God as the consummation of the old idea of the city of the gods, but far outshining it. John may have been saying this to these eastern people: "Here is the city of God of which you have always dreamed." What, then, can we say may be a summary title for beatitude number six? It is this: "In God's service, through Je-

sus Christ, there is perfect freedom: and in perfect submission to Him, there is complete victory for living."

9. Beatitude No. 7: A comment should be made concerning the verse (Rev. 22:15) which follows this beatitude. It reads as follows: "Outside are the dogs and sorcerers, and fornicators and murderers, and idolaters, and every one who loves and practices falsehood." The modern reader cannot get the force of the reference to dogs. Dogs are not loved as pets in many eastern countries. They run wild. As H. B. Swete states, "only those who have lived in these areas and have seen dogs prowl about wildly in the cities can appreciate the point here." The symbolism here for dogs is anything unclean and savage. There is a rabbinic saying like this: "Whoever eats with an idolator is the same as he who would eat with a dog. Who is a dog? He who is not circumcised." The meaning of this last word or beatitude is this: "Christ speaks as the great steward, who in the eventide of the world will call the laborers to receive their day's wages, but the deceitful person can have no fellowship with God, who is the God of Truth."

5

Glossary and Comments on Words and Comments on Revelation

1. "Bowls" (RSV) "Vials" (KJV) (16ff.) is translated "flasks" in the Living Bible; Good News Bible uses the word "bowl."

2. "The seven bowls of the wrath of God" (Ch. 16ff.): Cf. with ten plagues in Egypt, when Moses confronted pharaoh with the wrath of God and when he would not let the people go: (1) Water made into blood (Exodus 7:20–25), (2) Frogs (8:5–14); (3) Lice (8:16–18); (4) Flies (8:20–24); (5) Murrain on the cattle (9:3–6); (6) Boils and blains (9:8–11); (7) thunder and hail (9:22–26); (8) locusts (10:12–19); (9) darkness (10:21–23); (10) the slaying of the first-born (12:29–30): Compare this list with the terrors which follow the sounding of the seven trumpets: (1) Coming of hail, (Rev. 8:7); (2) Flaming mountain cast into the sea (8:8); (3) Fall of star Wormwood into the waters (8:10–11); (4) Smiting of one third of the sun, moon, and stars (8:12); (5) Coming of stars (9:1–12); (6) Loosing of four angels (9:13–21); (7) Announcement of final victory (11:15).

3. "Harlot": Stands for Rome. It may also mean Dea Roma, the cult (17:5).

4. "Ten kings with ten horns": They represent the satraps

of Parthia whom the resurrected Nero, the Antichrist, is to lead against Rome.

5. "Twenty-four elders": They represent the twelve patriarchs and the twelve Disciples. They also represent the totality of the Church. (See, e.g., Revelation 19:4.)

6. "Four living creatures": They are the lion, ox, man and eagle. They stand for the bravest, strongest, wisest and swiftest in nature. They are the cherubim. (See, e.g., Revelation 4:7.)

7. "Seven golden lampstands": They may be identified with the seven stars or planets, with the seven guardian angels of the seven churches, and with the seven churches themselves.

8. "Sharp two-edged sword": This represents the Word of God.

9. "Nicolaitans": Little is known about this group—if they were an organized one. They seem to have advocated some forms of idolatry.

10. "Seven horns of the Lamb": This expression stands for great and complete power.

11. "The Lamb": Imagery of Christ.

12. "Rider of the white horse": Represents conquest.

13. "Rider of the red horse": Represents civil war.

14. "Rider of the black horse": Represents famine.

15. "Rider of the yellow horse": Represents death.

16. "Sealing of the martyrs": The early Church pictures this sealing with the rite of baptism and the gift of the Holy Spirit (7:1–8).

17. "144,000" (7:4 and 14:3): This represents the future martyrs of the Church. They are the ones who will be able to come through the tribulation.

18. "Palm branches" (7:9): This is a symbol for victory.

19. "Blood of the Lamb" (7:14): This expression stands for all Christ did for us and means for us in His life and in His death.

20. "Three woes": (9:1–11:18): (Woe no. 1, "Pit of Abyss opened"; Woe no. 2, Release of Four Angels, Two Hundred Million Horsemen, Strong Angel with Little Book, Times of Gentiles; Two Prophets; Woe no. 3, "Worship in Heaven."

21. "Wormwood": Source of this word is unknown but, John may have remembered the suggestion from Jeremiah 9:15 who warned that his people will have wormwood and gall to drink because they had idols to worship. Wormwood is the fruit of idolatry in Deut. 29:17.

22. "Armageddon": Moffatt and a few other N.T. Writers spell the word, "Harmagedon." Armageddon means "the city of Megiddo." The meaning of Harmagedon means "mountain of Megiddo." It is most likely that the latter form is right, yet the plain would seem the place for a battle not a mountain. However, Ezekiel (38:8,21; 39:2,4,17) gives a description of the last struggle of victory being won in "the mountains of Israel."

And it may be John here describes the region near Megiddo in the Plain of Esdraelon where many battles were fought. Yet, the meaning of this word for us in the 20th century would be that the final battle between the forces of good and evil will be won by the former.

23. "Babylon" (17:5, etc.) It means Rome.

24. "Ten heads" (17:9): It means Rome.

25. "Ten horns which are ten kings" (17:12): They are the Parthian satraps, uncrowned governors, who will be reincarnated Nero's generals. (See Daniel 7:7.)

26. "Bottomless pit": This is not Hades, Sheol, Hell or Gehenna. It is a region where evil spirits dwell under a ruler called Abaddon (Hebrew), or Apollyon (Greek).

27. "Antichrist": The Antichrist represents the champion of every evil force found in the world. It also may stand for Nero reincarnated.

28. "Two witnesses" (Rev. 11:4): Two witnesses are the two lampstands and two olive trees who are to prophesy. Some have identified them with Moses and Elijah. Others see the two as Law and Prophets; still others as Law and Gospel. Two witnesses have been allegorized as the Church. Probably they are Moses and Elijah.

29. "Trumpets": The use of trumpets to symbolize the beginning of the new epoch of "last things" is tradition. See Isaiah 37:13 and Matt. 24:31.

30. "The woman with child" (12:1ff.): She is not Mary

mother of Jesus, but she represents the people of God from among whom the Messiah comes.

31. "Hatred of the dragon" (12:3): H. B. Swete finds in this picture the symbolism of an eternal truth situation. It is a struggle of forces of evil against man. (Cf. Jeremiah 51:34.)

32. "The flight to the desert" (12:6): This is to represent the Church fleeing to the desert.

33. "Woman escaping upon the wings of an eagle" (12:14): This is the symbol of the up- bearing arms of God. (Cf. Exodus 19:4.)

34. "The beast of the sea" (13:1ff.): This is the Roman Empire.

35. "The beast from the earth" (13:11–18): This second beast represents the priesthood of the imperial cults which organized and also supervised the worship of the emperor gods.

36. "666 or 616": The number of the beast (13:18). If we take the word Nero in Latin (Neron) and give it its numerical equivalent, we get this: N-50; E-6; R-500; 0-60; and N-50. The total is 666. If we spell Nero without the "N" the number is 616, which is in some manuscripts.

37. "Hallelujah" (19:6): is a word formed from two Hebrew words to mean "Praise ye the Lord," or "Praise the Lord." The King James uses the word "Alleluia."

38. "Marriage of the Lamb": This is the concept of divine marriage found in many passages of the O.T., e.g., Isaiah 54:4–6; 62:5; Ezekiel 16:6–14; and Hosea 2:19–20.

39. "Diademss" (Rev. 19: 12): This is a sign of royal power.

40. "The word of God" (Rev. 19:13): Is the conquering Christ.

41. "Millennium" (Rev. 20:4–6): It means 1,000 years. Another term may be used, "Chiliasm" which comes from the Greek word, chilios, meaning 1,000. The most common form of Millenarianism teaches that for 1,000 years before the final end, Christ will reign upon this earth in a kingdom of His saints. Many in the early Church held this view. After this reign, there will come the final struggle, the general resurrection, the last judgment, and the final consummation. This is the only place in the entire New Testament that this doctrine appears.

42. "Resurrection" (20:4ff): There seems to be two resurrections. The first one is for those who died and suffered for the faith. This is after their death. There is a second one, a general one, not to take place until after the 1,000 years reign of Christ. Special privilege is given for martyrs.

43. "New heaven and new earth" (Rev. 21:1): The present earth will be destroyed by fire. (Cf. Isaiah 65:17) "New Jerusalem" (Rev. 21:2) may be compared with the picture of hopes found in Isaiah 60:11–22; Haggai 2:7–9; Ezekiel 48:31–35, and Tobit 13:16–17.

44. "God" (Rev. 21:5–6): The only time God speaks to John is in this passage. H. B. Swete makes this comment: "The words are as true as they are tremendous."

45. "Foundations of the walls of the Holy City" (Rev.

21:5–6): This description should be compared with the passages in Exodus 28:17–21 and 39:10–14.

In the LXX, these twelve stones of the foundation also adorn the dress of the king of Tyre, according to Ezekiel 28:13, while in the Hebrew text nine are listed. In Exodus, each stone was engraved with the name of one of the twelve tribes. Whereas, in Exodus, the stones are engraved with the names of the twelve tribes, in Revelation they adorn the twelve foundations and are inscribed with the names of the twelve apostles (21:14).

46. "The Great Invitation": (Rev. 22:17) The invitation is in three parts: (1) The Bride and the spirit say: Come, means that Christ and His Church join in the invitation to accept all that Jesus Christ has to offer. (2) Come, those who have received the word must pass it along to others. (3) Come, the longing of the soul can now be completely fulfilled.

47. "Christian persecution in Rome": Roman historian Tacitus wrote: "All human efforts, all the lavish gifts, of the emperor (Nero) and the propitiations of the gods, did not banish the sinister belief that the conflagration was the result of an order. Consequently, to get rid of the report, Nero fastened the guilt and inflicted the most exquisite tortures on a class hated for their abominations, called Christians by the populace. Christus, from whom the name had its origin, suffered the extreme penalty during the reign of Tiberius, at the hands of one of our procurators, Pontius Pilatus. A most mischievous superstition, thus checked for the moment, again broke out not only in Judea, the first source of evil, but even in Rome, where all things hideous and shameful from every part of the world find their center and become popular. Accordingly, an arrest was first made of all who pleaded guilty. Then, upon their information, an immense multitude was convicted not so much of the

crime of firing the city, as of hatred of mankind. Mockery of every sort was added to their deaths. Covered with the skins of beasts, they were torn by dogs, and perished, or nailed to crosses, or were doomed to flames and burned, to serve as nightly illumination when daylight had expired. . . . It seemed not for public good that to glut one man's cruelty that they be destroyed.

6

Lesson One on the Revelation

1. The word "apocalypse" means the unveiling. Here is a definition of apocalypticism: "It is an eschatological (doctrine of last things) belief that the power of evil (Satan in most instances); who is now in control of this temporal and hopelessly evil age of human history in which the righteous are afflicted by his demonic and human agents is soon to be overcome, and his evil rule ended by the direct intervention of God: who is the power of good, and who thereupon will create an entirely new, perfect, and eternal age under His immediate control for the everlasting enjoyment of his righteous followers from among the living and the resurrected dead."

2. The Bible contains a number of small apocalypses. Examples are Joel 2; Isaiah 65; Amos 5:16–20; Amos 9:11–15; Zechariah 22–14; and Ezekiel 38–39. In the New Testament there are a few instances of apocalypses. They are Matthew 24 and 25; Mark 13; Luke 21; I Thessalonians 4; and I Corinthians 15.

3. One of the earliest records of the Revelation may be found in Justin Martyr (100–165), who lived in Ephesus. About A.D. 135 he wrote: "And, further, a man among us named John, one of the Apostles of Christ, prophesied in a Revelation made to him that they who have believed our

Christ will spend a thousand years in Jerusalem, and that afterwards the universal, and in one word, eternal resurrection of all at once, will take place, and also the Judgment."

4. Among the first Christians to reject a literal interpretation of the Revelation was Origen (185–254). He gave the book an allegorical interpretation. He rejected completely chiliasm (doctrine that Christ would return in a thousand years). Bishop Dionysius of Alexandria also rejected the literal view. He wrote a two-volume book on "PROMISES" in which he pointed out that the style of the Revelation is not like John's Gospel. He was bishop in Alexandria between 247 and 264.

5. Professor E. F. Scott in his commentary on the Revelation has observed the similarities between Caesar worship and Christianity. He says: (1) Both tried to promote a universal religion; (2) Both believed in the incarnation of the divine in human form; (3) Both were of recent origin and had to compete not only with traditional cults, but still more with each other; (4) Both claimed to conifer similar benefits on mankind and to deserve their allegiance; (5) Finally, both found the center of their system in the adoration of one whom they called, "Lord."

6. Three general answers are given to the authorship of the Revelation. The traditional answer is that it was written by the Apostle John. Most early first and second century writers take this view. Because of the Greek style, a second group says it was written by John the Elder perhaps of Ephesus. A third answer is that we don't know the author or authors. A common date given for the writing of the Revelation is A.D. 95. Scholars try to find the period of history which might correspond to an emperor's behavior. Emperors were: Tiberius (14–37); Gaius (37–41); Claudius (41–54); Nero (54–68); Galba; Otho (68); Vitellius (68–69); Vespasian (69–79); Titus (79–81); Domitian

(81–96); Nerva (96–98); Trajan (98–117); Hadrian (117–138); Antoninus (138–161). The usual date for the Revelation is during the reign of Domitian.

7

Lesson Two on the Revelation

1. The first three verses in Revelation 1 form a kind of preface such as are found in Old Testament books. Verse 1 shows that John wanted to let his readers know the true source of this book. Verse 2 gives John's own guarantee of the validity of this book. In verse 3 we find the first of seven beatitudes in the Revelation, the others being Revelation 14:13; 16:15; 19:9; 20:6; and 22:7,14.

2. The Greek word for "Revelation" is "Apocalypse." In Greek it is "apokalupsis." The word means "unhiding, the taking away of a veil, a revealing." Originally it was not a religious word.

3. These first three verses give us a concise account of how revelation comes to men and women. (1) It begins with God. (2) God gives this Revelation to Jesus Christ. (3) Jesus, as the writer of the Revelation says (1:1) He sent the truth to John through His Angel. (4) Finally, the Revelation is given to John. (5) It may be added that the content of the Revelation came quickly.

4. This passage (Revelation 1:1–3) ends with a three-fold blessing: (1) those who read these words are blessed. (2) Those

who hear these words are blessed. (3) Those who keep these words are blessed.

5. Revelation 4–8 might be called "The Prologue. Greetings." It also forms a second introduction to the book. The number seven chosen means completeness, perfection, totality. It was a sacred number probably because of the Sabbath on the seventh day. "Asia" was coterminous with, i.e., had the same boundaries as, the empire of the Seleucids, the Greek dynasty that flourished in the last three centuries B.C. By Roman times, it was identified with the Pergamene Kingdom when in A.D. 129 the possessions of Attalus III passed into Roman hands.

6. In Revelation 1:4, we read about God, the Father, and Jesus Christ but instead of the Holy Spirit, we have "the seven Spirits which are before His throne." These seven Spirits are also mentioned again in Revelation 3:1;4:and 5:6. Three explanations have been offered: (1) "The seven white ones" from I Enoch 90:21; (2) The passage from Isaiah 11:2 which offers the conception of the sevenfold gifts of the Spirit; (3) Finally, in Hebrews 2:4, we read of God giving "gifts of the Holy Ghost."

7. John tells us that when he had these visions he was on the island of Patmos. Unanimous tradition of the early church believed that John was banished to this island during the reign of Domitian (81–96). Jerome (340–420) says that John was banished in the fourteenth year after Nero (37–68) and liberated on the death of Domitian. Patmos is a small rocky island about fifty miles off the coast of Asia Minor. It belongs to the islands called Sporades. It is ten miles long and five miles wide.

8. Revelation 1:10–11 contains the first reference about the Lord's Day. In the Didache (Teaching of the Twelve Apos-

tles) written about A.D. 150, we read: "On the Lord's Day we meet and break bread." (14:1) Ignatius of Antioch, writing to the Magnesians (9:1), describes the Christians as no "longer living for the Sabbath, but for the Lord's Day." By the early part of the second century, we know that the Lord's Day had been accepted by the Christians.

9. Revelation 1:15–18 is the picture of the Risen Christ. It must be pointed out that each of the letters to the seven churches, which follow in Revelation 2 and 3, with the exception of Laodicea, opens with a description of the Living Christ, taken from this passage.

10. SUMMARY: Revelation 1:5–20. Verse 5, "It is a dependable message." Verse 6, "The love which will not let me go." Verse 7, "There is a visible Lord." Verse 8, "Origin and conclusion of everything is with God." Verse 9, "Power of the Christian faith is always found when man meets God." Verses 10–134, "The Divine Person: Christ is the Divine Person in human flesh." Finally, Verses 14–20, "Perfect Illumination of life."

11. LETTER TO EPHESUS (2:1–7): Ephesus was the chief city of Asia Minor. Apparently in verses 2 and 3 John is paraphrasing Paul's commendation of the Church at Thessalonica (I Thess. 1:3). John praises the Ephesians for their "works, toil . . . patience." Ephesus was associated with Emperor-worship. It was a city in which Jews were granted full citizenship and were given the right to their own customs. Ephesus was notorious for the practice of magic—maybe something like the rage over lotteries in Ohio. Paul in his last speech to the elders of the church at Ephesus (Acts 20:17–38) said that there would be "savage wolves" who would distort the message.

12. LETTER TO SMYRNA (2:8–11) We do not know when the church at Smyrna was founded, but we do know that it was a church of importance in the second century. While Rome and Carthage were fighting each other, this city built a temple to the goddess Roma. From the time of Tiberius (14–37), it was the center for the worship of the emperor cult. This city was called "the ornament of Asia." Lucian called it "the fairest of the cities of Ionia." The city stood at the end of a road which crossed Lydia and Phrygia. It was the city of rich commerce. The famous Bishop of Smyrna was Polycarp. He was martyred on Saturday, February 3, A.D. 155. John calls the Jews "a synagogue of Satan." Six slanders were made against Christians: (1) They drank blood (The Lord's Supper); (2) They held orgies (Agape feast); (3) They tampered with family relations (the faith split families); (4) They believed in more than one God (Christ was worshipped too); (5) They were disloyal citizens (they worshipped Christ instead of Caesar); (6) They were maliciously-minded people (they foretold the world would end in flames). Smyrna today is the Turkish city of Izmir.

13. LETTER TO PERGAMUM (2:12–17) The King James Version calls the city "Pergamos." Since A.D. 29, when the goddess Roma and emperor Augustus had been active in the promotion of the cult religion, this city became the center of worship. Although this city could not equal either Ephesus or Smyrna in commercial power, it did surpass both these cities in general culture. It had a very famous library. This library had over 200,000 parchment rolls. The word "parchment" is derived from Pergamum. In the third century B.C. a Pergamene king called Eumenes was important in the promotion of making these rolls from papyrus. Pergamum had two famous shrines. It also was, and considered itself, the guardian of the

Greek way of life and Greek worship of the gods. Here, too, was the worship of Asciepios, the god of healing. R. H. Charles in his commentary calls Pergamum "the Lourdes of the ancient world." Furthermore, Pergamum was the administrative center of the Roman Empire.

14. LETTER TO THYATIRA (2:18–29): The longest of these seven letters was written to the least important city of all. Pliny, in his letters, dismisses this city as a very unimportant city. The city lies between the valleys of Hermus and the Caicus rivers, through which a railway runs today. The importance of Thyatira is that it was the gateway to Pergamum, and Pergamum was the capital of the province. Jezebel, among the evil things she did, may have promoted emperor worship. Here is a church that was a center of activity. What is "the morning star" in verse 28? It may be taken as the promise of the first resurrection. It may be the conquest of Lucifer. It may reflect Daniel 12:3. The promise is, "They that be wise shall shine as the brightness of the firmament; and they that turn many to righteousness as the stars forever and ever."

15. LETTER TO SARDIS (3:1–6): Sir William Ramsey, in his book, on the letters in this book had this to say about Sardis. "No greater example may be found of the melancholy contrast between past splendour and present decay." Sardis was the ancient capital of Lydia. An earthquake struck the city in A.D. 17. However, Tiberius assisted in its recovery. Sardis stood at the midst of the plain of the valley of the River Hermus. The wealth of Sardis was legendary. The proverb "As rich as Croesus" was an expression about a former king. John in his introduction in this letter describes the Risen Christ in two phases. He (Christ) is He who has the seven Spirits of God. We found this reference in Revelation 1:4. It denotes the Holy Spirit with His seven-fold gifts, an idea found in Isaiah 11:2. It

also denotes the Spirit of His seven-fold operation. The second phase is that Christ is He who has the seven stars. The stars stand for the churches and their angels. The church is the possession of Christ. In any decision regarding the church, the decisive factor must be, not what any person wishes the church to do, but what Jesus Christ wishes to be done. The accusation against the church is that it is dead. The effect of sin is a kind of death. Sin is the death of will. It is the death of feelings. It is the death of all loveliness. In short, only by the grace of God can we escape the death of sin, and rise from that death, when sin has come into its power.

16. LETTER TO PHILADELPHIA (3:7–13): Philadelphia was a newer and lesser city without any special distinction. Apparently a wine center, its chief deity was Dionysus. An earthquake damaged it in A.D. 17 and was rebuilt by Tiberius. Its name was changed to Neo-Caesarea, but Nero restored its old name. This letter is to reassure Christians in their faith. It is similar to the one written to Smyrna. The Risen Christ in this letter is given three titles: (1) The Holy One; (2) The True One; (3) The Key of David. The Risen Christ has set before the Christians an open door which no one can shut. What is the meaning of this door? (1) It is a door of missionary opportunity. (2) It is a door none other than Jesus Christ. (See John 10:7,9.) (3) It is a door to the Messianic community. (4) It is a door for any person praying. Verse 9 states that some day the Jews will come and kneel with them for Christ. Verse 12 contains the promises to the faithful: (1) They will be the pillar in the Temple of God. (2) They will find life of untroubled goodness. (3) Jesus Christ will write upon the faithful Christian the name of His God. (4) They, the faithful, will have the New Jerusalem written upon them. (5) Finally, upon the faithful Christ will write His own Name.

17. <u>LETTER TO LAODICEA</u> (3:14–22): Laodicea is the arrogant church. This church is the least faithful and receives the strongest criticism. There were seven cities by this name. This one was on the Lycus River. The city had four characteristics: (1) It was a banking and commercial center. (2) It was a manufacturing center. (3) It was a medical center. (4) It had a very large Jewish population. Jesus Christ is given three titles: (1) He is Amen (See Isaiah 65:16 and John 1:51, 3:3,5,11). (2) He is a true and honest witness. (3) He is the beginning of the creation of God. The condemnation of Laodicea is a little crude. Barclay translates verse 15: "I know your works; I know that you are neither cold nor hot. Would that you were cold or hot. So, because you are tepid, and neither cold nor hot, I will vomit you out of my mouth." Things which are cold can be appetizing. So can hot food. Tepid food has a nauseating effect. The Risen Christ, in this letter, condemns the attitude of indifference. One impossible attitude to Christianity is neutrality. As someone has remarked, "To be neutral to Jesus Christ is to be an obstacle to Jesus Christ." Jesus Christ works through people. Finally, the Risen Christ is saying in this letter, it is better not even to start on the Christian way than it is to start and then to slip and to drift into a conventional and meaningless Christianity of respectability.

The tragedy of Laodicea was that it was convinced of its own wealth, and blind to its own poverty. Laodicea prided itself on three things: (1) It prided itself on its financial wealth. (2) It prided itself on its clothing trade. Garments made in this city were known all over the ancient world. However, the Risen Christ says that Laodicea was "wretched, pitiable, poor, blind and naked." (3) Laodicea prided itself over an eye-salve. It was exported all over the ancient world. R. C. Trench, in his commentary on the Revelation, wrote: "The beginning of all true amendment is to see ourselves as we are" and for this city it was blind. Revelation 3:19 is a verse whose teaching runs all through scripture. "Those whom I love, I reprove and chasten; so be zealous and repent." Verse 20 is one of the most famous pictures of Jesus in the whole New Testament. "Behold, I stand at the door and knock; if any one hears my voice and opens the door, I will come in to him and eat with him, and he with me." This picture may come from two sources. First, the Christian must be like the person who is ready to open whatever is heard (Luke 12:36). When the signs come, the Christian will know that time is near (Mark 13:29; Matthew 24:33). There is another meaning to this passage. It may be a much better view to take this passage to mean the Risen Christ is expressing the appeal as a Person as lover of our souls. In Solomon's Song 5:2–6, we read, "It is the voice of my beloved that knocks saying, open to me my sister, my love, my dove, my undefiled." Here Christ is the lover unlocking the door of the hearts of his faithful. Here may we see a (1) pleading Christ; (2) a supping Christ of fellowship. One final observation must be given to this letter. We have a human responsibility. Christ knocks. We can answer or not. As R. C. Trench remarked: "Every man is lord of the house of his own heart; it is his fortress; he must open the gates of it," and he has "the mournful prerogative and privilege of refusing to open."

8

Lesson Three on the Revelation

1. We may summarize from our study of the first three chapters of the Revelation by the following: (1) John assumes that he is well-known in the Christian community. (2) The first vision of the book (1:12–16) gives three titles to Christ: (a) a reliable witness of God; (b) the first-born of the dead; (c) ruler of the kings of the earth. The seven golden lampstands in Rev. 1:12 may have their origins in (1) Exodus 25:31–37; (2) I Kings 7:49) and (3) Zechariah 4:2. John seeing the lampstands "like a son of man" goes back to the picture in Daniel 7:13. The picture of the Risen Christ may be found in the seven letters. Ephesus is the passionless church. Smyrna is the persecuted church. Pergamum is the tolerant church. Thyatira is the compromising church. Sardis is the dead church. Philadelphia is the missionary church. Finally, Laodicea is the arrogant church.

2. Revelation 4:1 through 4:11 form "The Adoration of God in Heaven": It may be pointed out that for John his world consisted of earth, Hades, bottomless pit, lake of fire, and a single heaven above. For other ancients, the world consisted of sun, moon, and five planets. This belief is found in I, II, III Enoch and other non-Biblical sources. The hymn, "HOLY, HOLY, HOLY," written by Reginald Heber is based upon Revelation 4.

3. The Second Introductory Vision (Rev. 5:1–14) is "THE ADORATION OF THE LAMB OF GOD." This is a complement to the first scene. The "four living creatures" in the previous chapter were identified about A.D. 150 by Irenaeus as "the man" was Matthew; "the ox" was Luke; "the eagle" was Mark; "the lion" was John. However, St. Augustine (354–430) suggested that Matthew was the lion; Luke the ox; Mark the man and John the eagle. The roll in chapter five might have been suggested by Ezekiel 2:9–10. It describes God's purpose of destiny.

> God is working His purpose out, as year succeeds to year;
> God is working His purpose out, and the time is drawing near—
> Nearer and nearer draws the time—the time that shall surely be,
> When the earth shall be filled with the glory of God, as the waters cover the sea.

Swete, commenting on Rev. 5:5, states that John was weeping, and his tears were unnecessary because human grief is often needless, and it springs from insufficient knowledge. Christ is the "Lion of Judah" going back to Genesis 49:9, and "The Root of David" going back to Isaiah 11:1,10. The "seven horns of the lamb" testify to great and complete power. (See, e.g., Daniel 7:7, 20 and 8:3.) R. H. Charles quotes Christian Rossetti for Rev. 5:7–14, "Heaven is revealed to earth as the homeland of music."

4. Chapter 6 begins with the opening of the seals. We must keep in mind the Jewish concept of time. They saw two ages: THIS AGE and THE AGE WHICH IS TO COME. Between these two ages, there was to come a time of judgment and of to-

tal destruction. Leading up to this time were signs of the end which John now describes. The first section of the visions, the King James Version makes a mistake. It translates 6:1, "COME AND SEE." It should be "Come." This is not an invitation to John to come and see; it is a summons to the four horses and riders one by one to come forward on the stage of history. The origin of the vision is from Zechariah 6:1–8. The White Horse is of conquest (6:1–2). The Red Horse represents civil war (Rev. 6:3–4). The Black Horse represents famine (Rev. 6:5–6); the Pale Horse represents pestilence and death (Rev. 6:7–8). When the fifth seal was opened, there were the souls of the martyrs. (6:9–11). The early church pictures this sealing with the rite of baptism and the gift of the Holy Spirit. Jesus left no doubt in the mind of his followers that suffering and martyrdom was to be the lot of all. (See Matthew 24:9,10 and Mark 13: 9–13). The "souls" in this passage (6:9–11) is taken from the sacrificial ritual of the Temple. To a Jew, the most sacred part of any sacrifice was the blood; the blood was regarded as being the life; and the life belonged to God, and to none other (See Leviticus 17:11–14).

5. Revelation 6:12 through 7:17 are eschatological events. Three things must be noted in Revelation 6:9–11: (1) Here we have the eternal cry of the Psalmist—the cry, "How long?" (2) The martyrs wish for the punishment of their persecutors. Tertullian, a few years later, would taunt the heathens by telling them he would see them burning up in flames more hot than they gave the Christians. (3) Finally, this passage is telling us that the martyrs must rest in peace until the number of martyrs is made up. John, in the sixth seal is using a familiar Jewish concept. The end of time would be marked by (1) an earthquake (CF. with Amos 8:8 and Ezekiel 38:19). (2) There would be falling stars. To the Jew this was a terrible idea. (3) There will be "the folding up of the heavens." (CF. Isaiah 13:3)

(4) There will be "the moving of the hills and of the islands of the sea." (CF. Nahum 1:5) There are two significant things to be seen in Revelation 6:15–17. In this time of terror there will be a universal fear. Verse 7 in this sixth chapter speaks of kings, the captains, the great ones, the rich, the strong, the slave, and the freed. This constitutes the whole fabric of human society. No one is exempt from the judgment of God. The second observation on this passage is that John sees people hiding everywhere when the day of the Lord comes. Here is a great truth. We have the instinct to hide when we sin. We may also note one last thing. William Barclay writes: "That from which men flee is 'the wrath of the Lamb.' " Here there is the paradox; we do not readily associate wrath with the Lamb; the Lamb normally stands for gentleness and kindness. But here there is laid down the great fact that the wrath of God is the wrath of Love. God's wrath is not the sheer destructive wrath of hatred, which is out to blast and to destroy. God's wrath is the wrath of love, which even in anger is out to save, to amend and to redeem the one it loves.

6. The general picture we find in Revelation 7 is that of John seeing the vision of the terrible things to happen. However, before the time of terror and devastation comes, the faithful will be sealed with the seal of God in order that they may survive. So in verse 9 John sees the faithful after the tribulation has passed and after they have come through it. So in this picture we see three elements in it. First, there is a warning. The tribulation is coming soon. Secondly, there is assurance. In that time of terror the faithful will suffer, but they still will be saved. In the third place, there is the promise. When they have come through that time, they will come to the bliss.

Verses 4–8 of the seventh chapter have given interpreters thousands of words of discussion. Those who are to be brought safely through the great tribulation are sealed upon their foreheads. The origin of this idea may be found in Ezekiel 9:1–7. The seal indicates possession. In the early church, sealing was associated with (1) baptism and (2) Holy Spirit. Two things may be said about the number 144,000. It stands for those who in the time of John are sealed and preserved from the tribulation which at that moment was coming upon them. As we can see in Revelation 7:9, they are to be merged with the crowd beyond counting and then drawn from all the nations of the world. The number 144,000 stands for a perfect number and for completeness and perfection. It is made up of 12 multiplied by 12—the perfect square—and then rendered even more inclusive by being multiplied by 1,000. The listing of the twelve tribes of Israel does not mean that this number is to be taken entirely in Jewish terms. One basic thought of the New Testament is that the Church is the real Israel, and that the national Israel has lost all its privileges and promises to the Church. Furthermore, it would be a bad mistake to stress the order given of the tribes in this passage. Yet two things here are important. (1) Judah comes first, thus supplanting Reuben, who was the eldest son of Jacob. That is simply explained, because it was from the tribe of Judah that the Messiah came. (2) Dan is not listed. This is to be explained in that Dan does not hold a high place as compared with the other tribes and is sometimes connected with idolatry.

In verses 9–10 of chapter 7, we have the beginning of the future blessedness of the martyrs. John says five things about them. (1) He offers encouragement. (2) The number of martyrs are beyond counting. This may be a memory of the promise God made to Abraham that his descendants would one day be as numerous as the stars (Genesis 15:5) (3) John uses a phrase he likes when he says that God's faithful ones will come from the ends of the earth— from race, tribe, people, and tongue. (4) It will be a victory that the faithful finally arrive in the presence of God and of the Lamb. (5) Finally, the shout of the triumphant faithful ascribes salvation to God.

The picture drawn in Revelation 7:11–12 is a series of great concentric circles of the inhabitants of heaven. On the outer ring stand all the angels. Nearer the throne are the twenty-four elders, and still nearer are the four living creatures. The white-robed martyrs are before the throne. The martyrs have just sung their shout of praise to God, and the angels take that song of praise and make it their own. The angels' song has several parts: (1) They ascribe BLESSING to God. (2) They ascribe GLORY to God. (3) They offer THANKSGIVING to God. (4) They ascribe HONOR to God. (5) They ascribe POWER to God. (6) They ascribe STRENGTH to God. There is no greater exercise in the life of devotion than to meditate on the praise of the angels; and, as we do so, to appropriate to ourselves everything that is in it.

Once again a comment must be made about translation. It is in Rev. 7:13–14. King James translates, "These are they who came out of great tribulation." A more correct translation is, "These are they who came out of THE great tribulation." The whole point of the seer's vision is that it is granted to him to see beyond that terrible times, and to see the glory which is to follow. It is the tribulation of the end of time, not just the tribulation in general. This passage has two ideas and pictures which are common in the Bible. First, the blessed ones are in white robes. Early Christians were often baptized in white robes. These robes are to symbolize the new Christian life. The other thought is that of uncleanness. Isaiah speaks of unclean things as associated with unclean lives. The Psalmist asked to be cleansed so he might be whiter than snow. (51:1–7). Here, then, in verses 13–14 we have John saying that God's love and grace promised, not only forgiveness for the past, but renewal and cleansing to live a clean life in days to come. This passage speaks of the BLOOD OF THE LAMB. To us blood indicates death and the blood of Jesus speaks of his death. Yet the Hebrews used blood to mean life. However, in the New Testament, the blood of Jesus Christ means both life and death. (I John 1:7; Romans 3:25; Ephesians 1:7). There are, therefore, four ideas in this passage (13–14). The first is the most important and the other three are additions to the main thought. (1) Sacrifice is something which is designed to restore an interrupted and lost relationship to God. God gives the Law; man breaches it. The work of Christ's death restores it when man accepts Him. (2) This work of Christ has something to do with the past. (3) The work of Christ has something to do with the present. (4) This work of Christ has something to do with the future. The blood of Jesus Christ stands for all that Jesus Christ did, and is, in His life and in His death, whereby we are liberated from the consequences of our past life, given a peace, and equipped with newness of life for the days which are ahead. Two ideas come from our discussion or Revelation 7:13–14. The blessed ones have washed their robes, so that their robes are white. White stands for purity and for victory. What does the phrase "in the power of the blood of the Lamb" mean? It may be a vivid way of saying that this purity and victory were won in the power and at the cost of all that Jesus did. Here is symbolically laid down man's part in his own salvation. How, then, can a man avail himself of the sacrifice of Christ? The answer is (1) through penitence; (2) through faith; (3) through using the means of grace; (4) through the Scriptures; (5) through the sacraments.

The last three verses of chapter 7 are lines of poetry. The RSV so translates them. Verse 15 might have the title, "The Service of God." Those who have been faithful will have the entry into the very presence of God. Jesus said: "Blessed are the pure in heart, for they shall see God" (Matt. 5). The Greek word for "to dwell" is SKENOUN, which comes from the word, SKENE which means "tent." The Jewish word

SHECHINAH means the visible presence of the glory of God. The Jew would know they didn't mean the same but sounded alike. So then, the word SKENOUN always turned the thoughts of a Jew to the word SHECHINAH; and to say that God DWELT in any place was to say that the glory of God was there. The real meaning of this verse 15 is that he who faithfully works and witnesses for God has always the glory of God upon his work; work when it is done for God is still clad with the SHECHINAH, the glory of God.

Verses 16 and 17 of chapter 7 offer a spiritual promise. This promise is found many times in the New Testament. (See John 6:35) (John 4:14) Here is the promise of the loving care of the Divine Shepherd for His flock. Both the Old Testament and other non-canonical books offer this picture. In the Old Testament a similar picture is found in Psalms 23:1; Isaiah 40:11; Ezekiel 34:23; 37:24. George Adams Smith describes the shepherd of Palestine with those of other countries: "With us sheep are often left to themselves; I do not remember to have seen in the East a flock without a shepherd. In such a landscape as Judaea, where a day's pasture is thinly scattered over an unfenced track, covered with delusive paths, still frequented by wild beasts, and rolling into the desert, the man and his character is indispensable." The functions of a Divine Shepherd are two: (1) He leads us to fountains of living waters. (2) He nourishes our bodies and comforts our hearts.

9

Lesson Four on the Revelation

1. What we call Act II of The Revelation is a description of God's purpose in history. Revelation 4:1–11 form "The Adoration of God in Heaven." Chapter 5 (verses 1–14) is the "Adoration of the Lamb of God." The trumpet is probably Christ, while the throne is a symbol for absolute power. The seven seal visions (6:1–8,6) describe the four horsemen: (1) White horse, conquest; (2) Red horse, civil war; (3) Black horse, famine; (4) Pale (Moffatt has livid) horse, death. The fifth seal is the lament of the martyrs. They are given white robes and told to wait until the roll of them is complete. The opening of the sixth seal brings a series of ominous cosmic phenomena: (1) Earthquake; (2) Sun turns black; (3) Moon turns bloody; (4) The stars fell to the earth like figs; (5) The sky vanished like it is rolled up like a scroll; and (6) Every mountain and island was moved from its place. These six seals lie between the victory of the Lamb predicted in chapter 5 and the saints in chapter 7. Chapter 4 celebrates God as the Creator, and chapter 5 adds that the Lamb, as well as Jehovah, is worthy to be worshipped. Chapters 6 and 7 ask the question: "Who is worthy to join that worship?" It is the martyrs and the sealed. The first four seals form a unit which can be distinguished from the last three. The first four have the living creatures command, "Come forth." Then a horse appears with a rider on it. Each of the four seals are given only two verses. The fifth seal takes

three verses while the sixth seal takes six. Neither has anything to do with living creatures. The seventh seal is not mentioned until chapter 8. Chapter 7 consists of (1) sealing of the martyrs; and (2) the glorification of the martyrs in heaven. After these two interludes, the seventh seal is opened for the seven trumpet woes.

2. Revelation 8:1 states there was "silence in heaven about one half hour" when the Lamb opens the seventh seal. It might be that this silence is to permit God to hear the praise of the saints and their prayers for justice. When the silence ended, John saw "the seven angels who stand before God." They are given seven trumpets. The angels may be the seven spirits mentioned in Revelation 1:4 and 4:5. In Jewish thought, it was the archangel Michael who made the prayer for the people of Israel. The angel stood before the altar. It was an altar of incense not of sacrifice. (See Leviticus 16:12.) It was made of gold, and was eighteen inches square and three feet high. After prayers to God, the angel filled the censer with fire from the altar and threw it on the earth. There were peals of thunder and flashes of lightening. The seven angels now were ready to blow trumpets.

3. The KJV has in Revelation 8:7, "and the third part of trees was burnt up and all green grass was burnt up." Best manuscripts read (RSV), "and a third of the earth was burnt up, and a third of the trees were burnt up, and all green grass." Seventh of ten plagues inflicted on Egyptians had fire and hail (Exodus 9:13–26).

4. When the second trumpet sounded, what appeared to be a great mountain burning with fire, was cast into the sea so that a third of it became blood, a third of the creatures in the sea were killed and a third of the ships were destroyed. This is

a combination of the first Egyptian plague in which the water in the streams was turned to blood. (See Exodus 7:14–25.)

5. When the third angel blew the trumpet, a great blazing star (probably a fallen angel) falls on a third of the rivers and on the foundations of water. We do not know the origin of Wormwood. However, in Jeremiah 9:15 the people are warned that God will give them wormwood and gall to drink to chastise them for turning to idolatry.

6. When the fourth trumpet sounded, a third of the light of the sun, moon, and stars darkened. This woe may be a variation of that of the sixth seal (Rev. 6:12–13), when the sun was totally eclipsed, the moon turned into blood and the stars fell from heaven.

7. There was an interlude in between with the eagle's warning in Revelation 8:13. The King James Version substitutes "angel" for "eagle" in this verse. This is incorrect. Eagles have spoken in apocalyptic writings as we read in II Esdras 11:7–9, where the eagle is a symbol of the Roman Empire.

8. When the fifth trumpet blew, another star fell from heaven to earth and was given a key to the opening of the bottomless pit; the star stands for an angel. This star is not a fallen angel, but is one carrying out God's will. The bottomless pit is not Hades or Sheol, but an underground place with a door and lock. In I Enoch 19:1 and 20:1, we read that Uriel is the archangel in control of the abyss. S. J. Case in his book, *Revelation of John* (1919), suggests that this picture of the abyss may have been inspired by the thought of a volcano with its smoke, fire, and fumes.

9. In verses 2 and 3a when the angel opened the shaft,

smoke rose up that the sun could not be seen. The plague of the locusts may have been inspired by the eighth plague in Egypt. (See Exodus 10:4–15) Yet these locusts were not ordinary ones. They could sting like scorpions. Whereas locusts of Exodus destroyed all vegetation, here the grass and trees were to be saved. For a period of five months those who did not have the seal of God upon their foreheads were to be tortured. We do not know the reason for five months' time.

10. In verses 7–10 of Revelation 9, John pictures the locusts as winged horses prepared for battle. They have human faces, long hair like a woman's, lions' teeth (see Joel 1:6), iron breastplates, and stings in their scorpion-like tails possessing power to torture for five months. They wear golden crowns to show their power.

11. Verse 11 of Revelation 9 tells us that these demonic locusts have a king over them who is designated as "the angel of the bottomless pit." Is this the star-angel with the key who opened the pit to release them? This is possible because in I Enoch 19:1 and 20:2 an archangel Uriel is named as archangel of the abyss. Yet this is not absolutely certain. The name given to him is Abaddon which means ruin or destruction. His Greek name is Apollyon. As for the Greek name Apollyon, in the LXX Abaddon is regularly rendered as APOLEA, "destruction." So that Apollyon is equivalent to Abaddon.

12. The phrase "the first woe has passed" in verse 12, chapter 9, is puzzling in connection with the entire series of trumpet woes, but if related to the eagle's warning of three to come, it should present no problem. The first of these is now over, but two more are to come.

13. The sixth trumpet plague (Rev. 9:13–14) seems to be a

variation of the fifth, especially of the second Scene of the latter (Vs. 7–11), and may have some connection with the four horses and their riders of 6:1–8. When the sixth angel blew his trumpet, a voice from the altar before God ordered him to release the four angels who were bound at the great river Euphrates. This order may be in response to the prayers of the martyrs in 8:3 before the sounding of the first trumpet.

14. In Revelation 9:15, the four angels who had been bound at the Euphrates were released. Are these four angels at the four corners of the earth who were told to hold back the four winds of heaven until the faithful were healed? (7:1–3). There may be a connection with the four horses and riders in 6:1–8. The four angels are angels of punishment.

15. The leaders of a vast host of supernatural cavalry in Revelation 9:16–19 had 200,000,000 in number. It was not the men, but the horses that were deadly. They had lions' heads, and they kill their quota of men by "fire and smoke and sulphur." King James Version has "Jacinth" a transliteration of the Greek. RSV reads "sulphur."

16: The closing verses (20–21) are very similar to Joel. Joel (2:12–14) gives the destruction and devastation in the wake of the locusts and presents an appeal from God for sinners to repent. Here in Revelation, John also mentions the locust-horses. However, despite the manifestation of God's wrath, those who remained alive "did not repent" of their sins, chief of which is idolatry, the worship of "demons and idols of gold and silver and bronze and stone and wood, which cannot either see or hear or walk."

17. As the opening of the seventh seal was delayed by two scenes in chapter 7, so the blowing of the seventh trumpet

must wait upon the scenes in 10:1–11:14. The tableau in chapter 10 is largely a rewriting of certain scenes in Ezekiel 1–3. Ezekiel tells how he saw the heavens open and a great cloud driven by a high wind which came from the north flashing with light and glowing with an inner fire. As it drew near, the cloud resolved into the throne of Yahweh. Yahweh himself, was something like a man, but far more glorious. From the loins up he appeared like a fiery amber, and from the loins downward like fire. God then commissioned Ezekiel to prophecy against the children of Israel. God commanded Ezekiel to eat the scroll. He did it and found the scroll sweet as honey. By eating it he became possessed with prophecies, so that his book is actually a reproduction of the heavenly one.

18. John, since the fourth chapter, has been writing as if he were in heaven. Now he shifts to the earth. Here, John sees "another mighty angel" coming down from heaven. Like Yahweh in Ezekiel 2:9, "he had a little scroll open in his hand." It contained the prophecy of doom. In 10:2b–3a, "He set his right foot on the sea, and his left foot on the land" to symbolize his mastery over the whole world. In 10:3b–4, "he called out, the seven thunders sounded." This reminds us of John 12:28–29, where the bystanders thought they had heard thunder. However, there is a closer resemblance to be found in Psalms 29:3–9, where there is a sevenfold voice of God.

19. John, in verses 5–7, has the angel make an announcement. It sometimes has been taken to mean, "Time shall be no more." However, it probably means that there will be no further delay. Paul once wrote that the hour had struck when a man of sin shall be revealed. (2 Thess. 2:3) This Scene is being set for the final contest.

20. Revelation 10:8–11 pictures the joy and the sorrow of

the messenger of God. We see that God's revelation is never forced upon man. He must take it as Ezekiel takes the scroll twice. In passages in the Revelation, we are about to see the appearance of the Antichrist. The Antichrist is the incarnation of evil. The New Testament and John had some predecessors to the Antichrist. (1) Babylonians had the story of creation of the world by Marduk. He was always fighting with Tiamat, the dragon who stands for primeval chaos. (2) There is Belial, or sometimes called, Beliar. Belial appears in the Old Testament as a synonym for evil. (3) There is Satan, the Devil. He is sometimes identified as Lucifer, the son of the morning. (4) There was the development in the Old Testament of the Messiah. That word is the same as Christ. Christ is Greek, while Messiah is Hebrew. (5) Several places in the Old Testament there are pictures of divine wars, such as Gog and Magog in Ezekiel 38. When we turn to the New Testament, we find little mention of the Antichrist in the Gospels. One of the main pictures of the Antichrist is in 2 Thessalonians 2. The idea of the Antichrist appears in the Letters of John. However, the fullest picture of the Antichrist is found in the Revelation. It is seen in more than one form. The Antichrist is a spirit of falsehood and seduces man from the truth.

21. Antichrist takes several forms in the Revelation. (1) In Revelation 11:7, there is the picture of the beast from the abyss. (2) In Revelation 12, there is the great red dragon, who persecutes the woman clothed with the sun, the woman who begets a man child. (3) There is in chapter 13 the beast with seven heads and the ten horns, which comes out of the sea, and the other beast which comes from the land. (4) In Revelation 17:3, we have the scarlet beast, with seven heads and the ten horns, on which the woman who is called Babylon is seated. One final comment should be made. Nero was held to be the most ruthless ruler of the Empire. When he died, a belief

spread that he would return. This haunted Christians. John, no doubt knew of this popular belief.

22. Chapter 11 is the vision of the things to come; It forms the second interlude before the seventh trumpet is blown. John develops further the theme of the victory of the martyrs. This chapter may be studied in five parts. Verses 1 and 2 is the picture of the measuring of the temple. Verses 3 through 6 is the preaching of the two witnesses who are heralds of the end. Verses seven through ten is the first emergence of the Antichrist in the form of the beast from the abyss, and the temporary triumph of the Antichrist, which results in the death of the two witnesses. Verses eleven through thirteen is the restoration to life of the witnesses, and the consequent repentance and conversion of the Jews. Finally, in verses fourteen through nineteen, there is a sketch of the final triumph of Christ, the thousand years of his initial reign, the final rising of the nations, the defeat of the nations and the judgment of the dead, and the final establishment of the Kingdom of God and of His Anointed One.

We find that in the first two verses of chapter 11, the seer is given a measuring stick. We find similar examples of measuring in Ezekiel 40:3,6; Zechariah 2:1; Amos 7:7–9. John in these two verses is not measuring a real temple, but this building is the Christian Church. The Christians are living stones. The Temple is the people of God. Church is founded upon the apostles and Jesus is the corner stone. The forty-two months is 1260 days by the Jewish calendar. This is a mystical number of years, according to Daniel 9:27; 12:7, during which the Syrians under Antiochus IV, Epiphanes, a kind of Antichrist, would desecrate the Temple.

Verse three is a brief episode which prepares the way for the appearance of the two witnesses clothed in sackcloth. They will prophesy for one thousand, two hundred and sixty days;

the three and a half years during which the Romans will be permitted to continue their evil rule, the period of the Antichrist.

The symbolism of the "two olive trees and the two lampstands" which are before God is borrowed from Zechariah 4:1–14. The septiform candlestick is identified as the eyes of God going to and fro about the earth, and the trees are quite probably Joshua and Zerubbabel, the anointed religious and civil leaders. John changes the seven-branched candlestick to two lampstands. John makes them the two witnesses who are to prophesy.

In verses five and six, the witnesses are not named, but we can reasonably guess that they are Elijah and Moses. It was Elijah who called fire down from heaven to consume the messengers of King Ahaziah (2 Kings 1:9–16). It was Moses who as God's agent, turned water into blood in the first Egyptian plague (Exodus 7:17). Both Jews and Christians in the first century believed that Moses and Elijah were residents of heaven. As residents of heaven, both of them would be in a position to know what was going on in this world.

Accordingly, Elijah and Moses appear as prophets of repentance in verse seven. They are "witnesses" and "martyrs." The Greek may be translated both ways. The demonic beast appears from the bottomless pit and he will make war and kill them. The beast here is the first of four of his kind in Revelation. The others are the dragon, or Satan (12:3); the beast with ten horns and seven heads (13:1); and the beast with two horns who spoke like a dragon (13:11). Although these beasts are different, they are all incarnations of Satan and all enemies of Christ and Christians.

Verse 8 states that the dead bodies lay unburied for the mystical number of three and a half days in the street of a great city. The King James Version states that Sodom and Egypt are viewed "spiritually." The Revised Standard Version translates, "allegorically." Martin Kiddle, in his commentary on the Revelation suggests that Sodom and Egypt are not a single city but constitute the evil "great city" of this world.

The two witnesses in their reincarnation become martyrs in verses nine through twelve. The whole non-Christian world rejoiced at their deaths. The great interest in this passage lies in the fact that the unbelievers were won by the sacrificial death of the witnesses and by God's vindication of them. Here is the story of the Cross and of the Resurrection all over again. If ever evil is to be conquered, and if ever people are to be won, it cannot be done by force. It must be by the acceptance of suffering for the name of Christ, and by waiting the ultimate vindication of God.

Revelation 11:14 through 19 is a forecast of things to come. This passage is really a summary of future events not yet discussed by John. First, there is the victory in which the kingdoms of the world become the kingdoms of the Lord and of His Anointed One. This is really a quotation of Psalm 2:2, and another way of saying that the Messianic reign has begun. This victory leads to the time when God takes His supreme authority (verse 17). That is to say, it leads to the thousand years of the reign of God. Furthermore, at the end of the Millennium, there was to come the final attack of all the hostile powers (verse 18). In verse 19 we come back to the present. Verse 19 is difficult because two things are involved in this vision. (1) The Temple is opened. The Ark of the Covenant is seen. This act means that now the glory of God is going to be fully displayed. That which was secret is going to be made revealed. Why is a special reference made to the Ark of the Covenant? The new covenant is not just with the Jews but with all nations who believe in Jesus Christ. So these verses represent a picture of the coming of the full glory of God, which is a terrifying threat to the enemies of God, but an uplifting promise to the people of God's covenant.

10

Lesson Five on the Revelation

1. A short summary of our four previous meetings is in order. Act I, Revelation 1–3, had a preliminary section to the whole apocalypse, (1:1–8) and an introduction to the septet (1:9–20). The seven prophecies to the seven churches follow in Revelation 2–3. Revelation 4 and 5 form the second septet with the opening of the seven seals. Here we find the rider of the white horse (conquest); the rider of the red horse: (civil war); the rider of the black horse (famine); the rider of the yellow horse (death). With the fifth seal there is a lament of the martyrs (6:9–11). There is the sixth seal opened with the cosmic woes. This is followed with the sealing of the martyrs (7:1–8) and their glorification in heaven (7:9–17). The third septet is Revelation 8:1 through 11:14. However, after an introduction (Rev. 8:1–6), the seven trumpets are sounded. The seventh trumpet seems to comprise all of the fourth septet (Rev. 11:6–14:20).

2. Revelation 11:19 through 15:4 has the theme, "THE SALVATION OF THE CHURCH." The blowing of the seventh trumpet (Rev. 11:15–19) is delayed by the interlude pictured in Revelation 10:—11:14. The entire Scene there is a duplication, with variations, of Revelation 4:8–11. In this interlude (11:1–4), John develops the theme of the coming victory of the martyrs. John measures the temple with a "rod" (RSV), or "reed" (KJV). The Scene is like that of Ezekiel

40:3–42, 20; 47:1–12. Revelation 11:2–3 paves the way for the appearances of the two witnesses. These two witnesses will "prophesy for one thousand, two hundred and sixty days" during which time the Romans will be permitted to continue their evils, the period of the Antichrist. The symbolism of the "two olive trees and the two lampstands" which are before God is borrowed from Zechariah 4:1–14.

3. The two witnesses in Revelation 11:5–6 are not named, but they are usually considered to be Elijah and Moses. Elijah called down fire from heaven. (See II Kings 1:9–16). Moses was associated with a destructive fire, for the seventh plague consisted of hail mingled with fire (Exodus 9:23). These two witnesses in their incarnation became martyrs (Rev. 11:9–12). A few scholars would suggest that Enoch might be one of the two witnesses. In Genesis we read: "Enoch walked with God" (Genesis 5:24).

4. Revelation 11:14–19 is a difficult passage. This passage may be viewed as a summary of all that is still to come. (1) There is a victory in which the kingdoms of the world become the kingdoms of the Lord and of His Anointed. (2) This victory leads to the time when God takes His supreme authority (Verse 17). (3) But at the end of the Millennium there was to come the final attack of all the hostile powers (Verse 18). In verse 19 we seem to come back to the present. There is a vision of the heavenly Temple opened, and the Ark of the Covenant. In short, this passage is a picture of the coming of the full glory of God, which is a terrifying threat to the enemies of God, but an uplifting promise to the people of God's covenant.

5. Chapter 12 is the picture of the woman and the dragon. This chapter should be read as a whole before trying to understand it. The RSV says: "great portent appeared in heaven, a

woman clothed with the sun, with the moon under her feet, and on her head a crown of twelve stars" (12:1). The KJV says: "a great wonder." She is a sign in that her appearance has significance for Christians undergoing persecution. She is the "Queen of the Heaven." This woman stands for that Ideal Community of the chosen ones of God. Out of that Community came Christ. It was that community which underwent the terrible persecution.

6. The red dragon with seven heads and ten horns (verse 3) may have been suggested by Daniel 8:10 and Jeremiah 51:34. This beast may have been a symbol of Antiochus IV Epiphanes who exalted himself above the skies. These stars may have been the righteous Jews who were persecuted and slain by Antiochus. The male child in verses 4 and 5 is the pre-existent Messiah "who is to rule all the nations with a rod of iron." This prediction may have been taken from Psalm 2:9. In verse 6, the mother flees into the wilderness. Here the woman is the heavenly personification of the Church. In II Esdras 9:38–10:59 a woman is represented as a heavenly and earthly Jerusalem.

7. The second vision (12:7–9) is Michael's victory over the dragon. The name "Michael" might mean, "he who is like God." Verses 8 and 9, for the first time, identifies the dragon as the Devil and Satan. Although the Devil deceives the whole world, his victory is not complete. The presence of the dragon in heaven may seem strange as we read it, but when we take into account beginning with verse 1, we may find it explainable. Other sources place him in heaven, such as Luke 10:18; Ephesians 6:10–12; I Enoch 40:7, and II Enoch 7 and 18. Although the battle in heaven is not described, the dragon is cast out.

8. There is a song of woe and rejoicing in the third vision (12:10–12). The singers are not identified. Since the reference is made to "our brethren," (i.e., the martyrs), it may be that the singers are also martyrs, not angels. Satan is to be conquered not only by the blood of the lamb, but also by reason of testimony of the martyrs who preferred death to disloyalty to God and Christ. Like the scroll of doom and destiny which John ate, the coming events were to be both sweet and bitter to the martyrs. Sweet because the time is short; bitter because in his wrath during the time that remains, he will bring woe upon the people of the earth.

9. The Scene in verses 13–17 finds the dragon cast to the earth. The woman represents the people of God, while the Church in its widest sense of God's Chosen People from the midst of whom God's Anointed One came. There is a certain symbolism here. The dragon can injure the child by injuring the mother. That is to say, to injure the Church is to injure Jesus Christ. When we injure and hurt the church in the help we might have given it, we injure and hurt Jesus Christ. The woman here escapes. John uses here two pictures from the Old Testament. The woman escapes on the wings of a great eagle. (See Exodus 19:4; Deuteronomy 32:11,12; Isaiah 40:31). In the second picture, there is the picture of the floods of water cast out by the serpent. (See Psalms 42:7; Psalms 32:6; Psalms 124:4.)

10. The fifth vision describes the beast from the sea (13:1–4). The seven heads in Revelation is symbolic of the Roman emperors. The beast combines the powers of the four beasts of Daniel 7. The four beasts of Daniel are for the Persian Empire, Babylon, Graeco-Roman Empire and Media. The horns were for Antiochus IV Epiphanes who was blasphemous to the Jews. This vision, as with others, must be viewed with

the background of Caesar worship. Caesar worship was compulsory for every Roman citizen. Verse 6 is a little difficult. It may mean, literally, that the power of the empire and the institution of Caesar worship is a blasphemy against God, or it may mean this: The beast is the Roman Empire. It may be that John is thinking of all ways, not just the ways in his own time, in which Rome had insulted God and the dwelling place of God. Verse 8 may have two different translations: "Those whose names have been written from the foundation of the world in the Book of Life of the Lamb who was slain," or "Those whose names have been written in the Book of Life who was slain from the foundation of the world." Either translation means that God has known His own since the beginning of the world and nothing can take Him from His care for them. Verse 10 is made up of two quotations. The first one is from Jeremiah 15:2. The second one is from Matthew 26:52. It, verse 10, means that man must accept what God has ordained. Christ's faith cannot be forced upon anyone. However, the weapons which Christians must use are steadfastness and loyalty.

11. Revelation 13:11–17 deals with the power of the second beast. It is the beast from the land. The beast is the organization of groups to propagate Caesar worship. This power, John is saying, produces signs and wonders such as fire from heaven. This beast brings about it the fact that those who will not worship it will be killed. Those who had given in to the worship of Caesar, which was demanded of them had on them the mark of the beast. This mark was on their right hand and on their forehead. This picture of the beast coming "out of the earth" may have had a survival of a tradition preserved in II Baruch 29:4 and II Esdras 6:49–52. "The mark of the beast" is a parody of a sacred Jewish custom. When a Jew prayed, he wore phylacteries on his left arm and on his forehead. The

phylacteries were little leather boxes with little scrolls of parchment inside them on which the following passages were written: Exodus 13:1–10; Exodus 13:11–16; Deuteronomy 6:4–9 and 11:13–21. To wear these phylacteries was a sign of a devout Jew. But what then was the mark of the beast? Simply stated, it may be a certificate of worship which a Christian received when he denied his faith and was false to his God.

12. No verse in the Revelation has been studied and debated as much as verse 18 of the 13th chapter. This is the number of the beast. It should be remembered that ancient peoples had no figures for numbers. They had to use letters. The number given in the RSV, KJV and many others is 666. Many names have been suggested for this number: The Pope; John Knox; Martin Luther; Napoleon; Dr. Kepler suggested Hitler. Here is how you find Hitler: Let A equal 100; B equal 101; C equal 102; D equal 103 and so on. Then we work out the following sum: H equals 107; I equals 108; T equals 119 L equals 111; E equals 104 and R equals 117 which add up to 666. However, many scholars see in 666 Nero's name. It is found in this manner: N equals 50; E equals 6: R equals 500; 0 equals 60 and N equals 50 which add up to 666. The name can equally well be spelled without the final N and if we omit the final N, the number will be 616. The number 616 is found in very few manuscripts. It is also interesting to note that in Hebrew, the letters of Nero Caesar also add up to 666. There is little doubt in the minds of most New Testament scholars that 666 stands for the Emperor Nero.

13. Chapter 14 begins the series of seven visions: Worshippers of the Lamb and worshippers of the beast (14:1–20). The first five verses is the first vision of the martyrs and the Lamb on Mount Zion. Micah, for one, prophesied that following the judgment of his day of wrath, God would summon the

faithful remnant to Mount Zion, where he would reign over them forever (Micah 4:6–8). Similar prophecies are found in Joel 2:32; Isaiah 11:9–12; 40:1–46:13. We have found the 144,000 in Revelation 7. The mark on a person in ancient times stood for five things: (1) Ownership; (2) Loyalty; (3) Security; (4) Dependence; (5) Safety. This 144,000 are men. Although C. H. Charles dismisses the number as a monkish interpolation, all of the oldest manuscripts contain these numbers. Perhaps the reference to the fact that they "have not defiled themselves with women, for they are chaste," means they were of spotless character and certainly martyrs.

14. The second vision is a description of the marvelous reward for the martyrs, which is followed by the first of three angelic proclamations. This is something like the crying out of a three- fold woe by the eagle in Revelation 8:13. Here is a stern warning by the angel who admonishes that all should "fear God and give Him glory, for the hour of His judgment has come." He, the Creator, should be worshipped and not the Emperor of Rome.

15. The third vision pronounces the doom of Babylon (Rome) by the angel (14:8). This description of Rome is common between the Testaments. The writer of II Baruch begins with, "I, Baruch, say this against thee, Rome" (2 Baruch 11:1). Here we may have the fusion of the picture drawn by John from Isaiah 21:9, "Babylon is fallen, and all the graven images of her gods hath broken unto the ground." The other passage is Jeremiah 51:7, where we read, "Babylon hath been a golden cup in the Lord's hand that hath made all the earth drunken."

16. The fourth vision contains the angelic condemnation of the worshippers of the beast (14:9–12). In chapter 13, John gives the warning about the power of the beast (Rome). Here

he is giving warning to those who fail in their trials. The Church at this time was battling for itself. If the individual yielded, the Church would die. Verse 11 reminds us of the passage in Isaiah 34:8–9 of the destruction of Edom with brimstone and fire, "Shall not be quenched night and day: The smoke thereof shall go up forever." Verse 12 has the same words of the oracle given in Revelation 13:10. Here is the call for the endurance and faith of the saints.

17. The previous verse (12) and this one (13) is the second of seven beatitudes for the Revelation. The first one was Revelation 1:3. Those which are to follow are in Revelation 16:15; 19:9; 20:6; 22:7, and 22:14. This fifth vision with its heavenly benediction of the martyrs teaches that there is rest for the faithful person. Here, as well as in Revelation 2:23; 20:12–13; and 22:12, we find the teaching of good works. "Blessed indeed, that they may rest from their labors, for their deeds (KJV has "works") do follow them." Martin Luther had great difficulty with the Revelation and his doctrine of justification by faith.

18. The sixth vision (14:14–16) is the picture of the Son of Man and the harvest. Were it not that he is called "one like a son of man," the heavenly being "seated on the cloud" would scarcely be identified as the heavenly Christ in His second advent, but would be considered as an angel, for His function here differs but a little from that of the angel in the next scene. However, since in Rev. 1:3 Christ is termed "one like a son of man," even though the description is substantially different, it is probable that John is now anticipating the second advent of the conquering Christ, which is given its proper place in greater detail in Revelation 19:11–21. After the appearance of the Son of Man, an angel came out of the temple. We could conclude that since the word "another" is used that the "one like a

Son of Man" is also an angel. Instead, as in verse 6, it is the equivalent of "an." This angel commanded the Son of Man to reap with his sickle for the hour had come.

19. The seventh vision describes the angel gathering the vintage (14:17–20). This episode is a doublet of the preceding one of the harvest, and like it was probably suggested by Joel 3:13. In this case it is an angel, not the Son of Man, who appears with a sharp sickle. Yet, their functions are the same. This angel came out of the heavenly temple showing that he too is an agent of God's wrath. According to the angelology of that time, angels presided over the forces of nature. In obedience to the heavenly command (verse 19), the angel swung his sickle on the earth and gathered the vintage which he cast into the great wine press of the wrath of God. The wine press was trodden outside of the city. What city? Probably it was Jerusalem. This symbolism is also found in Isaiah 63:1–6, which pictures God as a mighty warrior who will trample in the wine press the nations which oppressed Israel.

11
Lesson Six on the Revelation

1. The Revelation has six symphonic themes. They are faith, hope, and victory. These six themes may be summarized as follows: After the introduction (1:1–1:6) the first theme is the vision of the church on earth (1:9–3:22). The second theme is God's purpose in history (4:1–9:1). The third theme is the church in trouble (Rev. 8:2–11:18). The fourth theme is the church's salvation (11:19–15). The fifth theme is the world in agony (15:1–16:21). The sixth theme is the judgment (17:1–20:3). There is another theme which might be added to these six. In fact two more. The victory is found in Rev. 20:4–6 and 20:11 to 22:5. The epilogue is Revelation 22:6–20.

2. After the letters to the seven churches (Rev. 1:9–3:22), the opening of the seals (Rev. 4:1–9:1), the sounding of the seven trumpets (Rev. 8:2–11:18), the showing of the seven pageants (Rev. 12:1–15:4)) the pouring of the seven bowls (Revelation 15:5–16:11) presents the world in agony. This section might also be called "the plagues." Another title has been given to these chapters (15:1–16:21) i.e., "the seven visions of the bowls of God's wrath."

3. There is a series of calamities, the seven plagues of the bowls of God to ravage the earth. These are like the plagues in Revelation 6:1–8:6 of the seven seals. They are like the seven

trumpets in Revelation 8:7–11:19. Verse I is full of Hebraic phrases from the Old Testament. The same word is used here as used in Exodus 11:1–9 for plagues. In Revelation this word occurs fifteen times. It is always used in an eschatological sense. "Wrath" as used here and in chapter 16 is THUMOS rather than ORGE. This same word is used in the phrase "wrath of God" in Revelation 6:16.

4. In verse 2 we find the prelude to the seven trumpet woes prayers of the martyrs ascended to God. This was parallelled by the Song of Triumph which the martyrs sung before the throne. John saw what seemed to be "a sea of glass mingled with fire." This same idea is also found in Revelation 4:6. However, here it is described as being fiery red in color. It helps to identify it as the heavenly Red Sea. The martyrs have crossed it safely. (See Ezekiel 1:4 and 1:13 and 1:27.)

5. Revelation 15:3 and 4 is the song of the victors of Christ. The martyrs sing two songs. They sing the song of Moses. This song Moses sung after crossing the Red Sea successfully. This song is in Exodus 15:1–19. The other song is that of the martyrs. Two things stand out in this song. First, it is almost entirely composed of quotations from the Old Testament. (See Psalms 92:5; 111:2; 98:1; 139:14; 145:17; 86:9; 111:9; 86:9; and 98:2.) One other characteristic of this song is that it is not a song of victorious martyrs, but it is an outburst of praise to God. An excellent summary of this verse may be given in the manner H. B. Swete puts it: "In the Presence of God the martyrs forgot themselves; their thoughts are absorbed by the new wonders that surround them; the glory of God and the mighty scheme of things in which their own sufferings form an infinitesimal part are opening to them; they begin to see the great issue of the world-drama, and we hear the

doxology with which they greet their first unclouded vision of God and His works."

6. Verses 5 through 7 is a Scene unfolding in heaven in which John calls for the temple of the tent of witnesses opened and the seven angels come forth. This is a common title in the old Testament for the tabernacle in the wilderness. (See Numbers 9:15; 17:7; 18:2.) It is from this place that the seven avenging angels come forth. What is the symbolism here? The great thing that lay there was the Ark of the Covenant; the ark or chest which contained the tables of the ten commandments, the essence of the Law. These angels came out of places where the Law of God rests. They are coming out to demonstrate the righteous Law of God. They are coming out to show that the Law cannot be disobeyed. They are clothed in shining white robes, they are girt about the breasts with a golden girdle. Their robes are symbolic of three things: (1) Their dress is priestly dress. They are God's representatives among men, (2) Their dress is royal dress. These angels come forth with the royalty of kings upon them. (3) The gleaming white robe is the dress of one from heaven. We may remember that the only man at the tomb of Christ was clothed in a long white garment. (See Mark 16:5 and Matt. 28:3.) It was one of the four living creatures who hands them the bowls of the wrath of God. When we are thinking about the four living creatures when they first came on the Scene in Revelation 4:7, we saw that the first was like a lion, the second was like an ox, the third was like a man, and the fourth was like an eagle. At that time we saw that, while they are the cherubim, they may well symbolize all that is the strongest and the bravest and the wisest and swiftest in nature in the world. If that be so, it is fitting that one of them should hand the bowls of wrath to the seven angels. These bowls are to bring disasters to nature in the world. All nature,

all that God has made, serves the purposes, the plans and the designs of God.

7. Verse 8 of chapter 15 might be called the "unapproachable glory." The idea of the glory of God being symbolized as smoke or as a cloud is common in the Old Testament. In the vision of Isaiah of the Holy God, the whole house was filled with smoke. (See Isaiah 6:4) Further, the idea that no one could approach while the smoke and the cloud were there is also common in the Old Testament. This was true both of the tabernacle and of the temple. Of the tabernacle it is said: "Then a cloud covered the tent of the congregation, and the glory of the Lord filled the temple of the congregation, and the glory of the Lord filled the tabernacle; and Moses was not able to enter into the tent of the congregation, because the cloud abode thereon, and the glory of the Lord filled the tabernacle." (See Exodus 40:34–35.) At the dedication of King Solomon's Temple, we read: "And it came to pass that when the priests were come out of the holy place, that the cloud filled the house of the Lord, so that the priests could not stand to minister because of the cloud, for the glory of the Lord had filled the house of the Lord (I Kings 8:10–11). There is a double idea here in this verse. There is the idea that the plans and purposes of God will often necessarily be clouded and obscured to men, for no man can see into the mind of God. There is the idea that the holiness and the glory of God are such that man in his own right and in his own merit can never approach God. R. H. Charles gives this observation about verse 8: No man could come into the temple until the seven plagues of the seven angels have been completed. The temple is, so to speak, closed until the plagues have worked their judgment. Charles sees in that symbolic statement that no prayer of man to God, no approach of man to God, can halt the coming judgment. The righteousness of God is to go out in avenging justice, and there

is nothing that can be done to halt it or turn it back, until it has completed its purpose.

8. Chapter 16 describes the pouring out of the seven bowls and the seven plagues. Let us first examine and list the ten plagues in Egypt when Moses confronted Pharaoh with the wrath of God, and when Pharaoh would not let the people of God go. They are: (1) The water made into blood (Exodus 7:20–25); (2) The frogs (8:5–14); (3) The lice (8:16–18); (4) The flies (Exodus 8:16–18); (5) The murrain on the cattle (9:3–6); (6) The boils and blains (9:8–11); (7) The thunder and the hail (9:22–26); (8) The locusts (10:12–19); (9) The darkness (10:21–23); (10) The slaying of the first-born (12:29–30). In the next place, we will set out the terrors which followed the sounding of the seven trumpets: (1) The coming of hail, fire and blood, through which a third part of the trees and all the green grass are withered (Revelation 8:7); (2) The flaming mountain cast into the sea, whereby one third of the sea becomes blood (8:8); (3) The falling star Wormwood goes into the river (8:10); (4) The smiting of one third of the sun and the moon and the stars, whereby all is darkened (8:12); (5) The coming of the star who unlocks the pit of the abyss, from which there comes the smoke, out of which there come the demonic and terrible locusts (9:1–12); (6) The loosing of the four angels bound in the Euphrates, and the coming of the demonic cavalry from the East (9:13–21); (7) The announcement of the final victory of God, and of the rebellious anger of the nations (11:15). Finally we will list the terrors described in this chapter 16: (1) The coming of the ulcerous sores upon men (16:2); (2) The sea becomes like the blood of a dead man (16:3); (3) The rivers and fountains become blood (16:4); (4) The sun becomes scorchingly hot (16:8); (5) The darkness over the kingdom of the beast, and the agony of it (16:10); (6) The drying up of the Euphrates to open a way for the hordes of the kings of

the east (16:12); (7) The pollution of the air and the accompanying terrors in nature, the thunder, the earthquake, the lightning and the hail (16:17–19).

9. When the preparations for the seven trumpet woes had been completed, the seven angels "made ready to blow" their trumpets. Corresponding to this scene, now that the seven bowl plagues have been prepared, a loud voice from the temple "ordered the seven angels to empty the seven bowls of wrath of God upon the earth." The speaker is not named, but since it has just been announced that no one but God was to be in the temple until the seven bowl plagues were ended (15:8), the speaker giving the command can be none other than God Himself, who now is to take personal charge of this last series of seven woes. The plagues that follow are patterned after those preceding the Exodus from Egypt. However, in his dependence upon the account of the Exodus, John here has reversed the sequence of events, in which the safe passage of the Red Sea, celebrated by the triumphant song of Moses, comes after the plagues; in Revelation the crossing of the heavenly Red Sea by the martyrs, who then sing the victorious song of Moses and the Lamb, comes before the sequence of seven plagues.

10. Revelation 16:12 pictures the hordes from the East. This verse gives the picture of the drying up of the Euphrates. This opening will permit the entrance of the hordes of the East to descend upon the world. The old Testament uses many times the concept of waters drying up to express the sign and action of the power of God. (See Exodus 14:21.) It might well be that John in this verse is remembering a famous incident in history. Herodotus tells us that when Cyrus the Persian captured Babylon, he actually did so by drying up the Euphrates. The greatest threat to the Romans were the Parthians. Their

cavalry was the most feared in the world. Perhaps John was seeing that horde sweep over the Romans.

11. Revelation 16:13–16 presents some problems. The three unclean spirits, like frogs, came out of the mouth of the dragon, the beast, and the false prophet. The unclean spirits are the words which are spoken as evil, disrupting, anti-God influences upon men and nations. Now it is said that the unclean spirits, the evil influences, were like frogs. Frogs are associated in the Old Testament with plagues (Exodus 8:5–11). Frogs are unclean animals. Although not mentioned by name, they are included by definition in the list of unclean things in Leviticus 11:10. Frogs make a lot of noise. Augustine said, "The frog is the most loquacious of vanities." So, then, the frog came out of the mouth of the dragon, the beast, and the false prophet, which is to say that their words are like plagues. They are unclean. But who is the false prophet in verses 13–16 of Revelation? The answer is that he is the man who tries to introduce the worship of other gods, a person who tries to make others compromise with the state or with the world, a person who tries to seduce other individuals from the exclusive worship of God is always a false prophet.

12. Verse 15 of chapter 16 contains the third beatitude. Previous beatitudes are Revelation 1:3; 14:13. There will be in Revelation 19:9; 20:6; 22:7 and 14 the remaining beatitudes.

13. No word, except the number 666, has received so much attention as "Armageddon," or as Moffatt and the American Standard Version translated, "Har-Magedon." Psalms 2:2 says, "The kings of the earth set themselves, and the rulers take counsel together, against the Lord, and against His anointed." Here we have the forecast of this last battle and terrible one. Armageddon means the city of Megiddo. Harma-

gedon would mean the mountain of Megiddo. It is most likely this last one is correct. When Ezekiel was describing the last struggle with Gog and Magog, he said that the final victory would be won in the mountains of Israel (Ezekiel 38:8,21; 39:2,4,17). It may be true that when John spoke of the Mount of Megiddo, he did so to bring it in harmony with ancient prophecy. The likely view is that the word is Har-Ma-Magedon, and that it describes the region near Megiddo in the Plain of Esdraelon which had already been the Scene of such tremendous victories and defeats, and which was famous as one of the great battle-grounds, perhaps the most storied of all battle-grounds in Jewish history.

14. Revelation 16:17–21 pictures the seventh bowl vision. While John has maintained a certain parallelism between the bowl visions and earlier trumpet visions, there were certain incidents between the sixth and the seventh trumpets which are not duplicated in the bowl sequence. (Cf. 10:1–11:14.) On the other hand, certain events following upon the sounding of the last trumpet are paralleled by episodes in the seventh bowl scene. When the last and seventh bowl was poured out into the air, a great voice from the temple and from the throne, which no doubt is the awful voice of God Himself exclaims: "IT IS DONE." This corresponds to the loud voices from heaven which was heard after the seventh trumpet blast. God Himself had said that the plagues were finished, that everything was ready for the consummation of the apocalyptic drama.

15. In verse 18, chapter 16, there is no antiphonal by the twenty-four elders as in 11:16–18, but the phenomena following the vision of the ark when the temple in heaven was opened—lightening, loud noises, peals of thunder, earthquake, and hail (11:19)—are all repeated, save for the hail, in those that occur after God's voice was heard announcing the

end. However, the earthquake which happened this time was the greatest in the history of mankind.

16. Immediately before the seventh trumpet, just after the two witnesses had ascended into heaven, an earthquake destroyed one tenth of the great city and killed seven thousand people. (Cf. 11:13.) This greatest of earthquakes however, split the great city into three parts and destroyed the cities of the nations as well. This city is identified as great Babylon. (i.e., Rome and the Roman Empire). Thus the predictions of 14:8 and 10, that Babylon the great would fall; and that the worshippers of the beast "shall drink the wine of God's wrath, poured unmixed into the cup of his anger" reach complete fulfillment.

17. In verse 20 of Revelation 16, we read of the outstanding result of the earthquake, that every island fled away, and no mountains were to be found. This is puzzling since we saw back in Revelation 6:14b that this happened when the sixth seal was opened. This repetition is just one of the indications that the different series of plagues are not actually to be considered as following one upon another, but are probably to be regarded as differing versions of the same series of eschatological woes preparing the way for the end of this world and this age.

18. In verse 21 (Rev. 16), the "heavy hail" which concluded the list of phenomena resulting from the seventh trumpet blast is magnified in this scene, where it consists of great hailstones each "about the weight of a talent" (KJV). The talent, which varied in value, weighed about one hundred pounds. Although Pharaoh had given some evidence of repentance during the plague of hail (Exodus 9:27), these dreadful stones of supernatural origin and size which fell on the Roman persecutors served only to cause them to blaspheme God as in

verses 9 and 11. With these hailstones, the seven bowl plagues are completed. The end is at hand. Christ has signified this when he proclaimed in verse 15, "Lo, I am coming like a thief." God affirms it when He in verse 17 says, "It is done." We are now on the threshold of the consummation; but a number of woes are yet to occur before the final act of this cosmic drama is staged.

12

Lesson Seven on the Revelation

1. Several comments must be made before we examine Revelation 17–19:10, our assignment for tonight. When the city of Rome first began to be a political force, the development of the cult of Roma, the deified personification of Rome, occurred. This cult did not originate in Rome itself, but with the Italian cities which were allied with Rome and the Greek cities which had become more and more very dependent upon her. The citizens of these cities recognized a divine element in the increasingly important city of Rome, which they personified and worshipped as the goddess Roma. When Rome extended her sway to Asia and the East, this worship of Roma was soon introduced to these areas. The Smyrnians, for example, boasted that they had erected a temple to Roma before Carthage had fallen to the Roman power. It was natural that the cult of Roma would be associated with that of the ruler. The goddess became a tutelary divinity of this city. It was in 29 B.C. that temples were built by Octavian (63 B.C.–A.D.14) to DEA ROMA and DIVUS at Ephesus and Nicaea for the citizens of those cities. Temples to Roma and to himself were built in Pergamum and Bithynia. The remains at Pergamum can be seen today. (See Letter to Pergamum, Rev. 2:13.)

2. Verses 1–3 of chapter 17 form a unit. The purpose is to explain the final complete destruction on earth. The Empire

must be ravaged by the invaders from the East. When this is done, there will be joy in heaven—this joy will be described in chapter 19. The Old Testament more than once describes immoral persons as harlots. John says he was carried away in the Spirit to a desert. Ezekiel said, "The Spirit lifted me up and took me away" (3:14).

3. Verses 4 and 5 give a vivid picture of the great harlot (Rome). John might have found this picture in the temple prostitutes of Asia Minor. John might have known about the notorious Roman Empress Messalina. She was the wife of the weak Claudius who at night would go down to the public brothels. Juvenal (A.D.60–140), the Roman poet has written a most distasteful account of this Empress.

4. After John in his first vision gives a picture of the harlot (Rev. 17:1–6), he sees in his second vision the beast at war with the woman (Rev. 17:6–18). When John saw this woman carried by the beast, he was puzzled and he marveled. The angel explained what he was seeing. Earlier we saw in Rev. 13:14 the beast was satirized as "the beast which was wounded by the sword and yet lived." This was in contrast to the slain lamb that dies and yet lives forever (Rev. 1:18; 2:8). According to the angelic explanation, the beast that puzzled John "was and is not, and is to ascend from the bottomless pit and go to perdition." This description is an ironical parody of the title given to God in Revelation 1:4, "who is and who was and Who is to come" (cf. 4:8) refers to the Nero REDIVIVUS expectation, for the beast, like the demonic Nero had died, but is to return to life.

5. Verses 7 through 11 is John's picture of the reincarnation of evil. John may be projecting himself back into the reign of Vespasian (69–79). The five emperors are Augustus, Tiber-

ius, Caligula, Claudius, and Nero. The one who is, is Vespasian. The one who is to come for a short time is Titus. The one who is to be the equivalent of the head wounded and restored, who is to be Nero all over again, is Domitian (81–96), a man of cruelty. Lying behind all this imagery are three permanent valid truths. First, every person leaves in this world something which continues when he or she is gone. In the case of Nero, it was sheer wickedness. In the next place, in verse 8 (Ch. 17), we read that those whose names have not been written in the Book of Life will be dazzled at the coming of the evil one. There are always those who can be dazzled by evil. In the last place, in verse 11, we read that the beast is on his way to destruction. However great the success and the triumph of evil may be, it has in it the seeds of self-destruction. He who allies himself or herself with evil has necessarily chosen the losing side.

6. We examine Revelation 17:12–18. This passage speaks of the ten kings whom the ten horns represent. Who the ten kings are is uncertain. However, it is likely that they represent the satraps and the authorities of the East and of Parthia whom the resurrected Nero, the Antichrist, is to lead against Rome. Or, they may simply be the world powers which in the end will turn against Rome and destroy her. There are three things we should note in this passage. First, verse 10 gives us a picture of the ten horns rising against the harlot. They will turn violently against her who had been their mistress. The two things which they will do are both taken from the Old Testament pictures. They will devour her flesh. Secondly, they will burn her in the fire. (See Leviticus 20:14.) The great harlot is to be punished with a punishment which befits a woman who became a harlot, and who should have known far better. This meaning may be found in these words. Evil has in it a divisive power; evil destroys fellowship, allies in evil will in the end split among themselves, and will thus destroy themselves.

7. In the third place, verses 12 and 13, we find the ten kings making unanimous and common purpose with the beast. In the 17th verse, we read that God put this purpose into their hearts that His purposes might be carried out, and that His words might be fulfilled. This may, indeed, seem strange as we read it. These evil powers thought they were serving and working out their own purposes, but they were, in fact, working out the purposes of God. R. H. Charles writes: "Even the wrath of men is made to praise God." The truth behind this is that God never loses control of human affairs. Even those who are rebelling against Him can be said to be working out His purposes in working out their own destruction. Even the person who thinks that he has cast God off is still under the power of God. In short, God is always working things together for good.

8. After we have seen in vision one (Revelation 17:3–5) the woman on the scarlet beast or the harlot, Babylon the Great, (Rome) and in vision two the beast at war with the woman or the interpretation of the harlot and the beast, (Rev. 17:6–18) we now turn to chapter 18 where we find the third vision of John. Here is the angelic proclamation of Rome's fall (Rev. 18:1–3). In verse 1, we find that the angel was so bright that he made the earth light. The RSV says, "the earth was made so bright with His splendor" while the KJV translates, "made bright with His glory." We see in Ezekiel 43:2 there is the theophany when the earth shone with God's glory. Reasons for Rome's ruin are very briefly stated. First, it is because the nations of the world had "drunk the wine of her impure passions" (RSV). Secondly, it is that the "merchants" of the world had become "rich" by sharing "in the wealth of her wantonness." James Moffatt says that John at this point has built his story like a musical symphony. First, Rome fell because of her

evil acts. Then she fell because she induced all the nations of the world to be like her.

9. Revelation 18:4–20 is the fourth vision. It is the exultation and the mourning over the fall of Rome. This vision is divided into two main parts. The first is a paean of rejoicing over the fall of the city, representing the views of the persecuted Christians (verses 4–8). The second part (verses 9–20) is composed mainly of the mourning of kings, merchants and shipmasters. In response to the angelic proclamation, "another voice from heaven" is heard. This speaker may be either Christ or God (Cf. 16:1). Verse 5 states that just as in Jeremiah (51:9b) Babylon's judgment "reaches to heaven, and is lifted up even to the skies," so the sins of Rome "have reached to heaven," and "God has remembered her iniquities." In verse 6, we find that God is going to apply the lex talionis, the law of revenge. This idea may be found in Jeremiah 50:29. The Sibylline Oracles have a similar thought as found in verse 7. There we read (5:168–171), "Woe unto thee all unclean city of Latin land, frenzied and poison-loving, in widowhood, shalt thou sit beside thy banks; and river Tiber shall mourn for thee, his wife, that hadst a bloodthirsty heart and a godless mind." Despite her assurance, God will punish her with a variety of plagues in a day, which will consist in the mourning she was sure she would never experience, and for good measure "death and famine and fire" (verse 8).

10. We find in verses 9 and 10 three groups as mourning for the fall of Rome. The first group consists of the "kings of the earth." Compare this with Ezekiel 26: 15–17, where the kings and puppet rulers dependent on Rome mourned the destruction of Tyre. The merchants (verses 11–17a) mourn because "no one buys their cargo anymore." However, in Ezekiel 27:36, the merchants (apparently rival cities) hiss in scorn at

ruined Tyre. The description of the rich merchants who mourned Rome's ruin is comparable with the description of the trade of Tyre as found in Ezekiel 27:1–24, save the latter passage is much more detailed. Verses 15–17a describes the dirge in which the city is personified as is represented "in purple and scarlet" and adorned "with gold, with jewels, and with pearls," as was the harlot in Revelation 17:4. The third group of mourners consists of the seafarers. Again we find a similar picture in Ezekiel 27:25–34. Here we may find a lesson for ourselves today. The laments of these three groups was not about what really happened to Rome as a city. They were lamenting about themselves. It is a law of life that when a person places all his happiness in material things, he misses the greatest of all things—love and friendship, and fellowship with his or her friends.

11. Amid all this lamenting, there comes in verse 20 the voice of joy. This paean of joy might be an amplification of 12:12a. See also Isaiah 44:23 and Jeremiah 51:48. This verse represents the rejoicing of heaven and of the martyrs resident there over God's "judgment," which now has been visited upon Rome in retribution for her many sins. A few scholars think this verse is misplaced and should follow verse 24. However, its present position is appropriate since it provides a dramatic and striking contrast to the dirges of the mourners, forming a delayed conclusion, as it were, to the exultation of the heavenly voice in verses 4 through 8.

12. The fifth vision, which concludes chapter 18 of Revelation, is the picture of the final desolation. Dr. Martin Rist calls it, "The Millstone Thrown into the Sea and Final Dirge." In Revelation angels play a great part, not only in the preliminaries of the apocalyptic drama, but also in its concluding events. For the most part, Christ, like God, does not intervene

directly. In verse 21a, it was this symbolic Scene of the actual destruction of Rome that another angel took up a stone like a great millstone and threw it into the sea. This Scene is patterned after the symbolic act related in the oracle against Babylon, taken from Jeremiah 50–51, which John had previously used. In John's adaptation of this prophetic symbolism, Seraiah becomes a mighty angel; the scroll weighted with a stone is a large stone like a millstone. The Euphrates becomes the sea. Babylon becomes Rome. The Seraiah's prophetic prediction of the fall of Babylon becomes an angelic pronouncement of the apocalyptic doom of Rome.

13. Let us examine verses 21b and 22a and b. The threnody of the angelic counterpart of Seraiah, which is contained in verses 21–24, is one of the best examples of poetic writing in Revelation. The opening words are an echo of those ascribed to Seraiah the traveler. The angel predicts that Babylon (Rome) will be overthrown. In verses 22a and b, John amplifies Ezekiel's oracle against Tyre. (Ezekiel 26:13; also see Isaiah 24:8). When we examine verses 22c and 23b, we find these lines are a free rendering of a verse from Jeremiah's prediction of the destruction of Judah and her neighbors by the Babylonians as God's agents of punishment. "Moreover, I will take from them the voice of mirth, and the voice of gladness, the voice of the bridegroom, and the voice of the bride; the sound of the millstones, and the light of the candle." (See Jeremiah 25:10.) The causes of Rome's destruction and desolation are given once again in verses 23c and 24. One reason is wealth and power of the merchants. (cf. verse 3.) The second is given as the real deception of all peoples by her sorcery. Sorcery is not defined, but from a study of previous passages in Revelation would include idolatry, fornication and murder. (See 9:21; 21:8; 22:15.) However, the main cause for the impending doom of Rome is the re-

sponsibility for the shedding of the blood of prophets and of saints.

14. A General Observation on the Last Four Chapters of Revelation. Chapter 19 begins with the universal rejoicing at the destruction of Babylon, the great harlot, the power of Rome (Rev. 19:1–10). There follows the description of the emergence of the white horse and on it, Him who is Faithful and True (Rev. 19:11–13). Next comes the assembling of the hostile powers against the conquering Christ (Rev. 19:19). Then comes the description of the defeat of the opposing forces, the casting of the beast and of the false prophet into the lake of fire, and the slaughter of the rest (Rev. 19:20–21). Chapter 20 opens with the binding of the devil in the abyss for a period of a thousand years (Rev. 20:1–3). There follows the resurrection of the martyrs to reign with Christ for a thousand years, although the rest of the dead are not yet resurrected (Rev. 20:4–6). At the end of the thousand years, Satan is again loosed for a brief time. There is the final conflict with the enemies of Christ. They are destroyed with the fire from heaven, and Satan is cast forever into the lake of fire and brimstone (Rev. 20:7–10). Then comes the general resurrection and the general judgment (Rev. 20:11–14). Finally, there is the description of the new heaven and the new earth and the new Jerusalem to take the place of the things which have passed away (Rev. 21:1–22:5).

Thus here are the final events, leading up to the final blessed for God's faithful and dedicated Christians. The final destruction for the enemies of God and the powers of evil is accomplished. Now there is the blessedness of the new world, and the old has passed away.

15. The first five verses of chapter 19 is the hymn of praise to God. It is the Te Deum of the angels. The first word is "Hal-

lelujah," which in Hebrew means "Praise ye the Lord." The KJV has "Alleluia." Although the word appears only here in the whole Bible, it occurs in a translated form frequently. It is the first phrase in Psalms 106, 111, 112, 113, 117, 135, 146, 147, 148, 149, and 150. The series of Psalms from 113 to 118 were called the Hallel, which means the "praise of God." They were an essential part of the education of every Jewish boy. God is here praised because salvation, glory, and power belong to Him. Each of these three great attributes of God should awaken its own response in the heart of any person. The glory of God awakens the reverence of a person. The power of God is always exercised in the love of God, and should, therefore, awaken the trust of man. Gratitude, reverence, trust—these are the constituent elements of real praise. Here God is praised because He has exercised His just and true judgment on the great harlot. Judgment is the inescapable consequence of sin. Thomas S. Kepler wrote: "The moral law can no more be broken than the law of gravity; it can only be illustrated." God is perfect in judgment for three reasons: (1) God alone can see the inmost thoughts and desires of a person. (2) God alone has that righteous purity which can judge without prejudice. (3) Only God has the wisdom to find the right judgment and the power to apply it. The judgment of God is the perfect judgment. The harlot was judged because she corrupted others. Someone wrote these lines:

All forbidden things we've sought,
All the mischief we have wrought,
All the sin to others taught,
Forgive, O Lord, for Jesus' sake.

There is another reason why the rejoicing and praise was being made to God in these first two verses of chapter 19.

There was proof that God had vindicated His people. God never in the end abandons His own.

One final comment must be made on these verses 1–5. Handel's great *Messiah* was produced in Dublin in 1742, and the "Hallelujah Chorus" was inspired by this passage.

16. The seventh vision consists of Revelation 19:6–10. It is the marriage hymn to the Lamb and His Bride. The description on verse 6a is like that of the singing by the 144,000 martyrs in Revelation 14:2. The songs here which follows (verses 6b–8), presumably by the martyrs, is the fourth in this series to begin with "Hallelujah," or its equivalent. The symbolism used here of marriage runs through the Gospels. (See Matthew 22:2; Mark 2:19; John 3:29.) R. H. Charles says that the marriage symbolism "denotes the intimate and indissoluble communion of Christ with the community which He has purchased with His own blood." This communion was also reached by the host of martyrs. Revelation 19:6–8 calls God a certain name. He is called the Almighty. The word is pantokrator, which literally means the one who controls all things, the one who has all things in His grip, the one whose power guides and directs all things. The word is used nine times in Revelation. It is a word peculiar to this book. Revelation 19:9–10 speaks of the marriage feast of the Lamb. Revelation 19:9 contains the fourth beatitude of the Book. (Previous beatitudes are 1:3; 14:13; and 16:15.) One final comment ought to be made about this passage (19:6–10). In verse 10, there is a repudiation of the worship of angels. This, we shall see, is repeated in Revelation 22:8–9. Paul had to warn the Gentile Christian community of Colossae against angel worship (Col. 2:18). Verse 10b is a reference to 1:9–11 where John explained that he "was in the spirit" when he received his prophecy.

13

Lesson Eight on the Revelation

1. We shall begin our last meeting with brief definitions of three topics: (1) Is Revelation an apocalypse or prophecy or both? (2) The Devil, or Satan; (3) Millenarianism. The relationship between prophecy and apocalyptic is very close. H. H. Rowley calls apocalyptic "the child of prophecy." However, Von Rad says this is not true. A difference between the two may be this. As a rule, prophecy is composed of brief, oral, and often poetic oracles which were proclaimed and then written later. Apocalyptic is a literary form from the beginning. Furthermore, it is longer and prosaic in its schematic construction. A difference on ethics is also detectable. While prophets had a profound interest in ethics, the apocalyptists did not. The greatest difference is their view of history. Prophets stood in their own generation and proclaimed righteousness, while the apocalyptists were very pessimistic about history. They took their stand in the remote past and looked at the future. Most of the apocalyptic writers were fond of using mythological motifs of the ancient world, while the prophets preferred historical thinking. Apocalyptists saw creation as the result of a conflict and spoke in terms of dualism. The prophets had confidence in God's world and God's role in it.

What are the similarities of Revelation as an apocalypse? (1) It is pessimistic about the world. (2) John foresaw a terrible end of the world. (3) There is a dualistic-eschatological explanation of the world. (4) John contrasts the present age of evil with that to come. (5) Mystery and secrecy are constantly displayed.

What are the differences between the Revelation and an apocalypse? (1) John's pessimism about man's history is overshadowed by his very optimistic, confident expectation about the ultimate outcome of history. (2) John's dualistic language has been modified by his strong monotheism. (3) John's deterministic element though present in Revelation, never suggests man's helplessness, nor does it threaten man's freedom or responsibility. (4) The mystery and secrecy in the Revelation is not like other apocalypses. Revelation does not have the esotericism which others have. (5) the Revelation is not pseudepigraphical. The author is John. (6) the Revelation reveals a different kind of suffering. In most apocalypses suffering results from decrees and acts of evil. In John, we find moral decisions can overcome suffering. (7) John has managed to retain the tension between human history and eschatological hope characteristic of the prophets and absent in most other apocalypses.

We may conclude that John, the writer of the Revelation, preferred that his work be known as prophecy even though it contained many elements of the apocalyptic.

2. The second topic which needs to be discussed is that of the Devil, or Satan. The word Devil means calumniator, accuser, or slanderer. The Greek word "diabolos" is a direct translation of the Hebrew word satan. In Christianity, the Devil is called Satan, Lucifer but less frequently Beelzebub, Belial, etc. In theological terminology, the Devil is regarded as the chief of the fallen angels. In the older books of the Old Testament, he is rarely mentioned. In the story of the Fall (Genesis 3) the serpent, which seduces Eve and is the cause of the first sin, has traditionally been regarded as the embodiment of

the Devil. The evil spirit tormenting Saul (I Samuel 18:10) has also been regarded as the Devil. The lying spirits that deceive the prophets of Ahab (I Kings 22:21–23) has been thought of as the Devil. In the Book of Job, Satan acts as a tempter, always in submission to the will of Jehovah. In I Chronicles 21:1, David's decision to *number* is attributed to Satan. In the vision of Zechariah, the Devil acts as the accuser of the high priest Joshua (Zechariah 3:1–2). The New Testament embodies and develops the later teaching of the Devil. The Devil tempts the Lord at the beginning of His ministry. (Mark 1:13; Matthew 4:1–11; Luke 4:1–13). Later we read where Satan renews his attacks upon the persons of the demoniacs, thus showing the enmity between his kingdom and the Kingdom of God. (See parable of the Tares among the Wheat in Matthew 13:24–30.) In John 16:11, Satan is judged after he has no power over Christ. At the last judgment, Satan and all who belong to him will depart into eternal fire. (See Matthew 25:41.) In I Peter 5:8–9, we find the suggestion of using sobriety and vigilance in resisting the Devil or Satan.

3. How has the Devil, or Satan, been interpreted by the Church? In the early centuries (A.D. 1–3), there was no fixed teaching about the Devil, or Satan. However, through the influence and popularity of the Book of Enoch, the view that demons are the sons of fallen angels and human mothers was held by many early Church Fathers. For example, Justin Martyr and others believed that we should distinguish between the serpent, the seducer of Eve, and the other fallen angels; and most of them held that the fallen angels was caused by their envy of man. Origen (185–254) rejected these tales from the Book of Enoch as his previous interpreters had made and attributed the Fall not to envy but to pride. Athanasius (920–1003) believed that the Devil (or Satan) was a spiritual being who fell from heaven through pride. Augustine

(354–430) believed that the Devil fell through pride because he would not submit to God, and that his envy of man was only a later consequence of his first sin. He also rejected the idea advanced by Origen that the Devil might be reconciled to God.

During the Middle Ages (476–1500), there was much speculation about the Devil, or Satan. The Dominican Order (founded about 1220) and the Franciscan order (founded in 1209 but taking more permanent form in 1223) gave two versions of the Devil, or Satan. The Dominican Order believed that all angels were created in a state of grace, though not of beatitude. The initial sin of the Devil, which fixed him in evil, was committed after the first instant of his creation had passed. It consisted of pride, showing itself in the desire not for the equality with God, which the angelic intellect knows to be impossible, but for the natural beatitude obtained by his own powers. The fall of the other angels was caused by their own consent to his sin. The Franciscans, on the other hand, following Duns Scotus (1264–1308), held that the devils, including the Devil or Satan, committed various kinds of sin before becoming obstinate in evil; that Lucifer, their chief, desired equality with God, and that his sin consisted of an immoderate love of himself. The Fourth Lateran Council in 1215 declared that the Devil, or Satan, became evil by his own will.

4. The third topic upon which some final comments must be made is that of Millenarianism. This is, of course, the belief that in a thousand years preceding the Second Coming of Christ, He will reign upon the earth in a kingdom of His saints, and at its conclusion take them with Him to Heaven. It is a Christian adaptation of conceptions of the Messianic kingdom on earth, such as were popular in the late pre-Christian Jewish apocalyptic speculation such as found in Daniel, 2 Esdras, and the non-canonical Book of Enoch. The millennial hope became popular in the second century A.D. Among those

who taught it were Cerinthis (about A.D. 100); Papias (60–130); Justin Martyr (100–165); Irenaeus (130–200); Tertullian (160–220); Montanus (about 172); Hippolytus (170–236); and Lactantius (240–320). Although Justin Martyr accepted the doctrine and found it in Revelation 20:4–5, he said many other Christians did not accept it. Lactantius gave a very vivid picture of the future. The heavenly bodies will give more light during the interim reign of Christ; the earth will produce food of its own accord; the mountains will drip honey; there will be streams of wine and water; all birds will live in peace. Just as Justin Martyr reported that some rejected this belief because it was too materialistic, the Didache (The Teachings of the Twelve Apostles) written in the middle of the second century predicted the reign of an Antichrist and the Second Coming of Christ. It did not mention a Messianic reign. Origen (185–254) allegorized the Millennium. He has a spiritual one in which he instructs all those capable of receiving Him, reigning in them until he has subjected them to the Father. Augustine (354–430) also allegorized Revelation. He said that there is to be no actual second advent of Christ before the final judgment, for His coming occurs continually in the Church and its members. The first resurrection is figurative, symbolizing the change in the status of people as they die to sin and rise to a new life. The thousand-year reign of Christ on earth actually began with Jesus Himself, for it is the Christian Church wherein the saints reign (*City of God,* XX.6–7).

The millennial hope has never died out. During the Reformation, the Anabaptists, as well as the Bohemian and Moravian Brethren, were Millenarians in the strictest sense; while in the seventeeth century there were Independents who held similar views. The Pietist Movement in Germany during the seventeenth and eighteenth centuries supported this belief. Bengel in 1770 wrote a commentary in which he placed the Second Coming at 1836. Irvingites, Mormons, Millerites

(Seventh Day Adventists), Russellites (Jehovah's Witnesses), are among the better known groups accepting this belief. Christians who believe that Christ will come before the Millennium are called pre-millennialists. Those who hold He will appear after the thousand years are post-millennialists. The *Oxford Dictionary of the Christian Church*, edited by F. L. Cross, concludes its discussion of this subject with this statement: "Though Millenarianism has never been formally rejected by orthodox Christianity, it may be doubted whether there is adequate justification for it either in Scripture or in the Christian tradition."

5. We begin today at Revelation 19:11 with the seven visions of the end of Satan's evil age and the beginning of God's righteous age. The series of seven visions each have ended. They have presented, with some repetition, a depiction of the evils and wickedness of this idolatrous age under the control of Satan culminating in the persecution and death of faithful Christians. The first of these seven visions is the picture of the conquering Christ (19:11–16). Before the marriage of the Lamb can take place, he must vanquish the enemies of himself and of his people. The conflict begins with Christ at the head of his forces and the Antichrist leading the nations of the earth. This is in addition to the Battle of Armageddon (16:12–16). It is also the conflict between the beast assisted by the ten kings from the East and the Lamb aided by the martyrs. (See 17:12–14.)

6. The second vision (19:17–21) is a description of the victory of Christ over the beast and the Antichrist. The description of this conflict is in part dependent upon the narration of the destruction of Gog and Magog in Ezekiel 39:1–20. In verses 19 through 21, the beast with his armies made war on Christ and His army of martyrs. Both he and the false prophet

(the pseudo Christ, whose last appearance was in 16:13, just prior to the battle of Armageddon) were captured and thrown into the lake of fire. Thus the reign of the Antichrist, of the satanic Roman emperors and empire, will come to an end. The Antichrist, symbolizing the priesthood of the imperial cult, will be tortured in the lake of fire forever. This fiery lake is not to be confused with Hades nor the bottomless pit. Instead, it is a place of eternal damnation and punishment for the wicked, the opponents of God and of the righteous, similar to the Jewish Gehenna, or the Greek Hell.

7. The third vision pictures Satan bound and his rule suspended for a thousand years (20:1–3). The reign of the Antichrist and of idolatrous Rome ended forever when the beast was hurled into the lake of fire. Satan is to receive the similar fate. John saw an angel descending from heaven holding a key of the bottomless pit and a great chain. He is probably the star angel of the Revelation 9:1 who fell from heaven and unlocked the bottomless pit with the same key so as to release the scourge of the demonic locusts. This time he had a more important task. Satan is to be kept here securely for a thousand years, after which he must be loosed for a short time.

8. The fourth vision (20:4–6) describes the reign of Christ— the millennium. John says he saw thrones and seated upon them those to whom the judgment had been given. This Scene might have been inspired by Daniel 7:9,27. Here thrones are mentioned in connection with the dominion given to the saints. These "thrones" in Revelation probably were occupied by the martyrs, a realization of the promises of Revelation in chapter 3, verse 21 that the conqueror would sit on the throne with Christ, and of the prediction by the four living creatures and the twenty-four elders that they would reign with Christ (5:21). Furthermore, it is stated that the millen-

nium is for but one group of people—the martyrs. Verse 5 tells us that the martyrs, and they only, are to share in the joys of the millennium. Others will not be restored to life at this time—only the martyrs. Verse 6 contains the fifth beatitude of the seven in Revelation. One fruit of the martyr is that he is exempt from the second death as is promised in Revelation 2:11.

9. The fifth vision (20:7–10) describes Gog and Magog being defeated and Satan being cast into the Lake of Fire, thus ending his age of control. This episode of Gog and Magog is based upon the popular idea that makes its earliest known appearance in a prophecy in Ezekiel 38–39. Accordingly, God will entice Gog of the land of Magog to attack and plunder the seemingly defenseless Israelites dwelling in the cities in peace and prosperity. Here John writes that when Satan was released (not God as in Ezekiel) Gog and Magog, the personifications of the "nations," were induced to besiege the "camp of the saints and the beloved city." In verse 10, as the beast and the false prophet had been captured and thrown into the lake of fire after their defeat by the conquering Christ, now, too, the Devil following the destruction of Gog and Magog whom he deceived "was thrown into the lake of fire and brimstone." There he was tortured forever.

10. The sixth vision (Rev. 20:11–15) is the final judgment. It is the disappearance of Heaven and earth. It is the second resurrection. This second resurrection is apparently physical, i.e., the souls of both the righteous and the wicked which went to Hades (Sheol) at death are not reunited with their earthly bodies. We find that in the main this belief in a physical resurrection was accepted in most of the apocalypses. Two kinds of books are mentioned in this passage. The first is the book which contains the records of the deeds of men. In Daniel 7:10 we read: "The judgment was set and the books were opened."

The second book here is the Book of Life. This concept often appears in Scripture. Moses was willing to be blotted out of the Book of Life if it will save the people (Exodus 32:32). We also find in this passage that at the time of judgment, the sea will give up its dead. The point here is twofold. (1) In the ancient world the burial of a body was necessary. If a body was not buried, its spirit would wander. Now these bodies from the sea will have a burial. (2) The bodies come from the sea and now cannot escape punishment with those who died in another manner.

11. The verses in chapters 21 and 22 are some of the most beautiful in the Bible. The "New Creation" is described in the first verse of chapter 21. John sees the vision of the doom of the wicked. He also sees the vision of the bliss of the blessed. Sorrow is to be forgotten. Sin is to be vanquished. Darkness is to be at an end. In verse 2 John draws the picture of the New Jerusalem. The New Jerusalem is the "bride" of Christ mentioned in Revelation 19:7–10. A more complete account will be found in verses 9 following of this chapter. The concept of the New Jerusalem comes from two sources: (1) The first is Greek. Plato taught, for example, that there was the present world, which is but a pale, shadowy copy of the heavenly realities. (2) The second source of this concept is Hebrew. In Haggai 2:7–9 we read: "The glory of the latter house shall be greater that the former, saith the Lord of hosts; and in this place will I give peace, saith the Lord of hosts." Revelation 21:2 and 3 promises the fellowship with God. God is to make His dwelling-place with men. The word used here is skene, which literally means "a tent." We find God speaking for the first time in Revelation 21:5–6, God is God who is able to make all things new. God says to John, "I am Alpha and Omega." This claim we read in Revelation 1:8. However, in verses 7 and 8, this bliss is not for every-

one. God condemns disloyalty, immorality, the worship of false gods, and blatant insincerity.

12. The city of God is described in verses 9 through 27 of the twenty-first chapter. It is interesting to note that the same angel in Revelation 17:1 who brought the message of destruction is the one who in verse 9 brings the message of bliss. What is this? It must be that John wishes us to see here that the servant of God does not choose his task; and that he must do obediently and willingly whatever God sends him to do; and that he must speak clearly and fearlessly whatever God gives him to speak. Now as the Holy City descends in verse 11, it is seen to possess "the glory of God." H. B. Swete sees a hint of Philippians 3:15 here, "Ye shine as lights in the world." The wall is about the city and has twelve gates with the twelve tribes of the sons of Israel on them. These gates, writes William Barclay, stand for the "catholicity of the Church." He sees the twelve tribes standing for the continuity of the Church. (Verse 12) When John begins to measure the city (21:15–17), he gives a picture not unlike Ezekiel 40:3. The city's shape is foursquare. The city is about 1,500 miles on each side with a total area of about 2,250,000 square miles. Such a city would stretch from London to New York City. This simply means that John is saying that the city is where there is room for everyone. The walls are about 266 feet high. Babylon's wall was 300 feet. The city is made of pure gold. The city has twelve foundations. Perhaps the best view of Revelation 21:19–20 is that the precious stones which were in the city are the same as the stones in the breastplate of the high priest in Exodus 28:17–21 and 39:10–14. In Exodus, the stones are engraved with the names of the tribes; whereas in Revelation, they adorn the twelve foundations and are inscribed with the names of the twelve apostles (verse 14). Verse 22 gives a unique feature of the city. There is no temple in it. The reason why the city does not need a temple is that the

presence of God and of the Lamb is continually there. Here is the explanation of the symbolism for this statement: Where God is, the Church is; where the presence of Christ is, there is the Church. The old Latin statement is true: Ubi Christus, ibi ecclesia, The presence of God and Christ make a Church, not buildings.

13. Revelation 21:24–27 demands special attention. Here is a picture of all the nations coming to God, and all the kings bringing Him their gifts and their honor. In short, here is a picture of universal salvation. Isaiah has a picture of the day when all nations will go up to Mount Zion to be taught the law and to learn the ways of God (Isaiah 2:2–4). There are three points which may be made from the study of chapter 21 and these last four verses of it. (1) More than once John insists there shall be no night there in the city of God. In the new world the dark will be no more, for the presence of God will bring eternal light. (2) Plato said: "The unexamined life is not worth living." We may add from John: The unexamined faith is not worth living. (3) Finally, chapter 21 ends with a threat. Those who will not lay aside evil of their ways are barred from the city of God.

14. The first five verses of chapter 22 describe the New Garden of Eden with the river and the Tree of Life. So far the description of the Holy City has been its exterior. Now we are to see the interior. First, there is the river of the water of life. This picture has many sources in the Old Testament. (See Genesis 2:8–16; Ezekiel 47:1–7; Joel 3:18; Zechariah 14:8.) There is the picture of the fountain of life in Revelation 7:17; 21:6. What is this symbolism? H. B. Swete definitely identifies the river of life with the Spirit. Swete would identify the river of life with the life-giving inflow of the Spirit coming from the throne of God and of the Lamb. It ought to be noted that in

this passage there is an ambiguity of punctuation. The phrase "in the midst of the city street" may be taken, not at the end of the first sentence, but with the words which follow, and as the beginning of the second sentence. It will not then be the river which is in the midst of the street, but the tree of life.

15. The final culmination of the description of the Holy City may be found in verses 3–5 of chapter 22. There will be no accursed thing there. God's servants shall see Him face to face. The promise of Matthew 5:8 that the pure in heart shall see God comes true. The sight of God produces two things: (1) It produces the perfect worship. (2) It produces the perfect consecration.

16. Verses 6 to the end of the chapter are disjointed and disconnected. There is no logical order. These verses form what the Interpreter's Bible calls "The Epilogue." The speaker in verse 6 may be Christ or may be the angelic guide. The verse is a guarantee of the divine inspiration of the book. "These words are trustworthy and true" were spoken by God in Revelation 21:5. If the angel is the speaker in verse 63, then Jesus interrupts to say, "And behold I am coming soon." The next sentence in this verse contains the sixth beatitude reminding those being in trouble that the end is near.

17. An interpretation of verses 10 and 11 of chapter 22 may have one of two suggestions. It may mean, there comes a time when it is too late to change. Or the passage may mean: Let each man do what pleases him; I will not force his choice. The Risen Christ appears again in verses 12 and 13. He makes two claims: (1) He has His reward with Him, and will render to every man according to his work. H. B. Swete writes: "Christ speaks as the Great Steward, who in the eventide of the world will call the laborers to receive their days' wages." (2) Christ is

the Alpha and the Omega. This is a repetition of phrases and titles used in 1:17; 2:8; and 21:6. There is here too the idea of completeness. There is the idea of eternity. There is the idea of authority. So, then, we have here in verses 12 and 13 of chapter 22 the symbols of the completeness, the timelessness, and the authority of Jesus Christ.

18. Verses 14 and 15 present a problem in translation. The Authorized Version (KJV) has, "Blessed are they who do his commandments." The RSV, Moffatt, and American Revised Standard Version have, "Blessed are they who wash their robes." The Greek of the two phrases would be very similar. "Those who have washed their robes" would be hoi plunontes tas stolas; "Those that do his commandments" is hoi poiountes tas entolas. If these Greek phrases were placed together in English letters they would look like this:

HOIPLUNONTESTASSTOLAS
HOIPOIOUNTESTASENTOLAS

Therefore we should read that those who have the right to enter into the City of God are those who have washed robes. There then follows a list of those debarred from the City of God. A new phrase in the list is dogs. The dog was a symbol of everything unclean and savage. John may have used it to mean all that is disgusting and unclean.

19. Revelation 22:16 contains the guarantee of truth. This book began by promising a revelation to be given by Jesus Christ (1:1). The revelation is, in fact, mediated by angelic messengers, given in visions, and brought through the Spirit. This is the guarantee and the attestation of Jesus Christ that, however the vision came, it came from Him.

20. Verse 17 of chapter 22 is the great invitation. We turn now from the picture of the future age to the plight of John's fellow Christians. H. B. Swete takes this verse to mean in its first part an appeal to Christ to fulfill His promise and to come quickly back to His world in His Second Coming. William Barclay, on the other hand, believes that the whole passage is a great invitation to all men to come to Christ, and to accept Him. Barclay suggests the verse has three parts: (1) First, the invitation of the Spirit and the Bride, the Bride being the Church. (2) The second section: "Let him that hears say: Come," demands of us to be a Christian missionary. The third part (3), is an invitation to all the thirsty souls to come to Jesus Christ that their need and their longings may be satisfied.

21. We find a very solemn warning in verses 18 and 19. This must not be interpreted literally because this book circulated outside of the Bible before it became a part of it. The Greek text is the poorest of all the books in the New Testament. This ending is not a unique ending since all ancient books usually ended with such a warning. (See Deuteronomy 4:2; Proverbs 30:5–6; and Enoch 104:10.)

22. The last words of Revelation in verses 20 and 21 have both pathos and glory. Come what may, John was sure of the grace of his Lord. He was equally sure that grace was sufficient for all things. It is surely symbolic, and it is surely fitting, that the last word of the Bible should be GRACE.